"Learn how to be in a sta~~ __ __~~ ~~~~~~ ~~~~~. ~~~~~ ~~ wnat you will absorb by reading *Fields of Plenty* by LD Thompson. Thompson guides you down a path of understanding the egoic mind versus the soul. He offers gentle solutions of how we can shift into the right side of the mind and, in doing so, live a happier and more fulfilled life. The lessons in this book will transcend the way you see and interpret things and fill you with a limitless feeling of bliss. The answers are all within. Discover the gift of being."

— Jen Grisanti, story/career consultant, author: *Story Line: Finding Gold In Your Life Story* and *Change Your Story, Change Your Life: A Path To Success*

"In *Fields of Plenty* LD Thompson has refined his message. The result is profound, restorative, and hugely consoling. It is an invaluable guide for those on a quest for self under-standing and spiritual growth. It is a wise and wonderful book."

— Judy Corbett, author: *Castles in the Air* and *Envy*

"*Fields of Plenty* is filled with practical explanations and meditations to anchor knowledge. It is a roadmap to an awakened life and a worthy successor to LD Thompson's first book, *The Message*. I highly recommend it for reading and practicing... I keep it next to my bed."

— Sabrina Fox, author: *Body Blessing*

"In *Fields of Plenty*, LD Thompson has given readers a simple yet complete operating manual for living a fulfilling life on all levels (physical, emotional, mental, spiritual). Within its pages you will be reminded of that which you know deep in your heart. Because this timely volume provides a clear roadmap to happiness, many readers will probably discover the next steps in their life journey."

— L. Steven Sieden, author: *A Fuller View* and *Buckminster Fuller's Universe*

"I was thoroughly enchanted reading *Fields of Plenty*. This book is an absolute gem and came to me at a time when I needed it most. It is filled with not only deep wisdom, but stories, tools, and techniques that make this an essential resource for personal growth and, yes, liberation. *Fields of Plenty* is one of those books that embodies a quality of grace that is, in itself, a great blessing."

— Robin Mastro, author: *Altars of Power and Grace* and *Making Room for Mr. Right*

"Readers will benefit from these startling quotes from Solano, which resonate as powerful touchstones throughout the book. The author's spiritual wisdom, both serious and playful, creates new footholds in the realm of spiritual thought, making distinctions between wisdom and fear, ego and soul."

— Stephen Lloyd Webber, author: *Writing from the Inside Out*

"I love *Fields of Plenty*! Through Solano's wisdom and LD's intuitive scribing of this profound material, the read is easy and rich. One can't help but to shift the paradigm for oneself even while reading as it instantly puts the reader in observer mode. From there, the reader will observe the old patterns as a well-trodden path of simply learned behavior. Use this book as a call to action, create a new path to feeling that sense of plenty that already is known to your soul."

— Joan Ranquet, author: *Communication with All Life, Revelations of an Animal Communicator*

"The tools, practices, and perspectives offered here serve as gateways to freedom, so we can experience ourselves abundantly as the radiant immortal self that we are!"

— Kiara Windrider, author: *Year Zero: Time of the Great Shift* and *Ilahinoor: Awakening the Divine Human*

fields of plenty

A GUIDE TO YOUR INNER WISDOM • LD THOMPSON

DIVINE
ARTS

Published by DIVINE ARTS
DivineArtsMedia.com

An imprint of Michael Wiese Productions
12400 Ventura Blvd. # 1111
Studio City, CA 91604
(818) 379-8799, (818) 986-3408 (Fax)

Cover design by JohnnyInk www.johnnyink.com
Interior Design by John Brenner and Gina Mansfield
Copyediting by Matt Barber

Printed by McNaughton & Gunn, Inc., Saline, Michigan
Manufactured in the United States of America

Library of Congress Cataloging-in-Publication Data

Thompson, L. D.
 Fields of plenty : a guide to your inner wisdom / LD Thompson.
    pages cm
 Includes bibliographical references and index.
 ISBN 978-1-61125-021-3 (alk. paper)
1. Spiritual life--Miscellanea. 2. Spirituality--Miscellanea. I. Title.
BF1999.T5158 2013
204'.4--dc23

                              2013015967

Printed on Recycled Stock

CONTENTS

ACKNOWLEDGMENTS

It is with humble gratitude that I acknowledge those who encouraged and refined, questioned and helped guide me in writing this book.

I wish to acknowledge David Rothmiller for being there tirelessly in every aspect of the book, from concept and substance to syntax and design. Your creativity is inspiring and I am eternally grateful.

To Sabrina Fox for her constant encouragement and valuable feedback. Anne Dagney Fox for her dedication and time working with the material. And to Thomas Sharkey for knowing that this is my path.

Heartfelt thanks to Robin and Michael Mastro for their ongoing support of my work.

I also want to thank my publisher, Michael Wiese, and his lovely wife Geraldine Overton — your mentorship and loving support is such a gift in my life. I am grateful also to the entire team at Divine Arts — Matthew Barber for your precision editing, positive feedback, and insightful questions which carried the book over the finish line; Manny Otto and Ken Lee for your skillful shepherding of the book; John Brenner for your inspired creativity; and Gina Mansfield for your care and artistry.

Thank you all from the furthest reaches of my Soul.

And, of course, wordless thanks to my benevolent teacher Solano, without whose wisdom, this book would not be.

plen·ty *n.* A large quantity or amount; an abundance

PREFACE

Fields of Plenty *is a guide to becoming conscious of what
you are manifesting in your life. In understanding what
you are manifesting and why, you open the doorway to
knowing deeply and fully your Soul's design for your life,
and to experiencing the "plenty" — the abundance — that
the Soul knows in every moment.*

*Do I present what I share here from the viewpoint of
an "expert"? An "enlightened" being? Not at all. I am a
teacher and counselor. Another human being here on
Earth. A work in progress. I have a spiritual guide, Solano,
whom I consult and whose wisdom I access. He is my
compass, and over the years he has become that for
many others. (In my book* The Message: A Guide to Being
Human *I describe my first meeting with Solano in detail
and how my life was forever changed.) Above all, I am a
student. I've gained some skills. I have more peace in my
life than I did when I was younger. But that doesn't give
me the ability to say that I am "enlightened." The day I
make that claim, I imagine, will be the day that my studies
here on Earth have concluded.*

What transpires when I am in deep meditation, my meeting place with Solano, is an access to wisdom far beyond my own awareness. Call the phenomenon what you will. (I characterize what I do as merging with Divine Mind.) Who or what Solano is becomes somewhat irrelevant to me, and is ultimately inconsequential to the information that I share with you here. What matters is that the wisdom is practical and grounded. Solano describes himself this way: "I am the One, just as each of you are the One. Everything that is emanates from One Source. There is no separation save in the creativity of each Soul who is exploring singularity."

This book's aim is to reveal your Soul's design for your life. If, as you read, you feel as if you are more awake, more empowered, have greater understanding and peace, if there is practical, employable value in these words and you are able to experience your life as more plentiful, then know that it is because of you. It is because you were ready to make a change toward improving the quality of your experience here on Earth.

The basic message within these pages is that we exist in abundance, for all the Soul knows is abundance — is "plenty." How to connect with that knowledge is what's to be learned. The Soul is eternal and infinitely intelligent, and from the Soul's standpoint, everything that we experience here is the pure potential — God — manifesting around us to fulfill the Soul's desire for wisdom.

You dwell in plenty this moment —
all your Soul knows is plenty.
— *Solano*

INTRODUCTION

Loss on any scale is a time to re-evaluate priorities. I have been working as a teacher and counselor for more than thirty years. I often help others deal with just such crises — the loss of a loved one, the loss of financial security, or simply the loss of a perceived self-identity.

But helping others does not inoculate me from the pain of my own experiences of loss.

I once had a most enchanting client. Her devotion to truth and spiritual development powered her desire for more interaction with me. As she navigated the troubling waters of career success and personal ambition, she came to rely on Solano's wisdom and the comfort of my counsel.

Our relationship grew past that of counselor and client. I was invited into her circle of friends and family. We had many moments of joy and celebration as her career blossomed. It affected my life both emotionally and financially. It was a heady time, but one that was also fraught with some attending drama, as her emotions were often fragile.

I felt honored to be included in her family, until long-suppressed family dynamics surfaced, bringing relationships into question. Suspicion and doubt soon colored her treatment of everyone in her support system, including me.

A new business manager suggested she reorder her team of advisors. And though I knew of her intentions and agreed with the need for change, I was ill-prepared when I received a letter of severance from any further business dealings.

We had just spoken the night before, and I offered what solace I could to help her through the harder parts of the changes. Her family members, once on the payroll, were all being cut off. She was tired and depressed, so she understandably cancelled our dinner plans.

The following day I called to discuss the letter and her phone number had been disconnected. And her email address had changed. I received no other communication from her and had no way to reach her. Many years have now passed.

Naturally, at the time, my experience of loss was profound. Yet, I needed to understand what there was for me to learn from it... lessons in letting go of identity and attachment, learning humility, and one of the tougher ones — overcoming the feeling of betrayal. But after I had gone through those exercises I knew there was more that I wasn't getting to, because I still felt deeply unsettled.

Shortly after this happened, I returned to the quiet and beauty of the Northwest. Needing a personal retreat,

I went to the San Juan Islands to collect myself and to better hear the answers to the questions I knew needed to be asked. My finances were now in jeopardy, as I had come to rely on work no longer offered.

The first morning sitting on the deck of Otter Cottage I watched as the sun rose over Pea Vine Pass. I dropped into a quiet meditation and asked for guidance.

Clearly, I heard Solano's voice, "My friend, dwelling in plenty is not about manifesting what you think you want. It's about understanding what you are manifesting because that is most truly what you are asking for, either consciously or unconsciously."

"You are saying I asked for this," I said, not without a little bitterness.

"Everything that manifests does so in accordance with your walking prayer — the consciousness that you inhabit. Your consciousness is the sum of several elements — your thoughts, your beliefs, your genetic blueprint (which is designed by your Soul) and your Soul's curriculum — what it aims to learn in any given lifetime."

"There's a lot of room in there for things that feel entirely out of my control," I replied.

"You could look at it that way, especially if you look at it through the eyes of the limited and acculturated mind. But if you identify with your Soul — who you are in your truest nature — you will see that the themes that you've been working with all of your life are all presented in this challenge. You felt you had arrived, in a manner of speaking. You lived far beyond the level of the accomplishments of your forebears. You began to feel powerful in an earthly sense. You allowed friendships and long-term alliances to fall away. You went into a kind of trance where the altered ego's fear of loneliness and isolation were far from your thoughts. Betrayal, being abandoned, being humiliated, being seen in a way that did not match your perception of yourself — all of these themes are in this challenge and they are all ones that you have been working with which are part of your curriculum in this lifetime."

"In other words," I said, "I've got my nose to the grindstone and I'm back in school again. The whole thing, though, makes me feel like I'm stuck in old patterns and doomed to repeat them over and over again."

His words were concise: "You are consciously back in your Soul's curriculum. You never really veered from it. You simply took a path that let you drop into a trance for a while. Most everyone does at some point. For example, when people fall in love and believe that they are no longer alone, only to find out that the object of their love is really just a mirror to show them where their own lack of self-love is, and where they lack understanding of their Oneness with the Divine. You are not hopelessly stuck. You are presented yet again with the opportunity to shift your consciousness."

Solano uses the term "Infinite Intelligence" to express the "Divine." He speaks of the "Divine Mind," "Divine Wisdom," "Source," "Universal Intelligence," and "God" interchangeably.

I sat up a little taller, "All right, then, I'm in school. This has my full attention. What I'd like out of this is the means to close all of the gaps that caused me to find myself in this situation."

Solano's words have always provided me with comfort and, often, with enthusiasm for what lies ahead. This time was no different. "That is appropriate. We will begin with the gap in the understanding of abundance. We will also explore emotions and love, genetics, the 'altered ego' and the way it is created, the way to identify, once again, with your Soul and how, ultimately, to integrate the altered ego and the Soul. Let us begin with the fundamental understanding of how your experience of reality comes into being...."

Becoming Soul-Identified

This moment, identify with your Soul.
View all things in your life from the Soul's perspective.
This moment, proclaim that your radiant Infinite
Intelligence, your Soul, is in command of your life.
— *Solano*

ALTERED EGO

The key to dwelling in plenty is to become Soul-identified. The way to achieve this is to accept that what you are experiencing is precisely what you want, to embrace what is. The Soul, because it knows it is forever and cannot be harmed, sees value in every experience. The altered ego is the part of you that judges some things as being less than desirable. Sometimes it cannot accept that what you are experiencing, you have created.

The altered ego is the aspect of your being that is built on fear. It activates your emotional body when you find yourself concerned about your mortality, concerned for your safety, concerned about getting your needs met in the form of comfort, food, safety, or companionship. When you find yourself in fear, in that moment you are identified with the body and therefore identified with the altered ego.

> *"Altered Ego"— the aspect of one's*
> *personality that responds to criticism and*
> *shaming; a defensive part of the persona.*

When you challenge a habit, or a fear that consistently causes you to stumble, or when you strive to move beyond a particular limitation, you begin the journey to becoming consciously Soul-identified.

When you become Soul-identified you understand that everything that you experience occurs right within you. Within, you are already fully and completely one with God, the Source. The extraordinary gift of incarnation as human allows you to explore the identity that comes from experiencing singularity here on Earth.

The Soul ordains everything that you experience.

— *Solano*

Every fear, limitation, struggle, addiction, every lack, every habit that you confront, is there because your Soul ordains it as part of the path to the wisdom it desires. Such altered ego inspired emotions result in the strain that marks most people's lives. Yet that strain is the very thing that leads you to freedom, because it instigates the search for understanding. If you consistently fear for your body's well being, if you fear death, when you face that fear and walk through it, what is on the other side? Always it is the exquisite freedom of discovering that you are immortal, invulnerable to any sort of pain or suffering and incapable of being destroyed.

You may know what it is like to be on the brink of an emotional reaction and to step back from it and the suffering that you know it will bring. Perhaps you have already experienced turning your attention to your Soul and discovering there a greater peace, grace, and creativity. That process is part of the arc of a mortal life.

As you follow this arc, recognize that the moments when you are called out by your Soul — when you experience fear or lack or disappointment in a relationship or dissatisfaction with your career — these are all instances in which the Soul is calling you out of your identification with the altered ego and is beckoning you to release that identity. As you are called to your greatest challenges, rather than trying to control them with the intellect, look at them with the eyes of the Soul and see the circumstance as something the Soul uses for your growth.

Fear is the grist by which wisdom is gathered.

— *Solano*

EMBRACING FEAR

Fear is your teacher and greatest means for gathering wisdom. When you experience fear, you have not stumbled, nor are you inept, or a coward. It signifies no lack of enlightenment. It is a tool for self-knowledge.

If you embrace your fears you have an opportunity to understand your Soul's design for this life. Every moment that you are called out by your Soul to a fear, or an addiction, you begin a process that ultimately leads you to the grace that you seek.

Once you acknowledge a fear, the process of creatively meeting that fear or that limitation begins. You have taken the most important step. You are operating from your Soul's guidance, not from your altered ego or your intellect. The Soul recognizes that any challenge put in its path, met creatively, expands the awareness and lifts the vibratory frequency of the individual. The energy of that creativity sparks each cell in your body, and that causes the magnetic field around you to vibrate at a higher frequency. This has the net effect of drawing to you opportunities, mentors, guides, and the very things that allow you to move with grace through the struggles that are presented.

If you have been struggling, you are not stuck there. Rather, you are once again being called to identify with your Soul. You can make that shift of identity when your altered ego relinquishes control as the body declines, or you can do it this moment by going through every fear or contraction or limitation. Regardless of which way you do it, acknowledge that such moments are the opportunities your Soul designs to provide you with the wisdom you desire in your life.

When you realize that everything you experience
is self-generated, energy leakage stops.

— *Solano*

ENERGY LEAKAGE

When you view yourself as being at the effect of what you perceive as external reality, you leak vital life force energy. That leakage causes a diminishment of vitality in the body. Remind yourself that there is nothing external. You will then find yourself approaching fear differently — starting a conversation that you've been afraid to begin, taking a journey that you have been afraid to take, revealing your authentic self to others — or to yourself, for that matter. It is then that you begin to move into the creative aspect of engaging your Soul's curriculum.

Recognize that everything you experience you have generated. Courageously face your own creation. Then the leakage of energy from the body that happens as a result of altered ego identification stops. You become full of your own radiant energy. You become fearless. You then settle down into your Soul.

An exercise to facilitate settling down into your Soul: Imagine that you are in a pool of water and your day to day, often limited, thoughts take place on the surface. Take a deep breath and slowly settle down to the bottom where it is still and calm.

You then arise each day centered, unaffected by the demands of your work, or the demands of relationship, or the conflicting demands of a complex world. You know what is true for you. You know what kindness is. You know what it is to be loving, truthful, and compassionate. You know what it is to dwell in your Soul's values. Open. Generous. Fearless.

The challenge is maintaining that consciousness moment to moment. It is possible to become so anchored in the awareness that you are a radiant immortal being that you never lose that exquisite peace.

There is nothing external.

— *Solano*

Take a moment and imagine that everything that you have ever experienced, everything that you know, everything you see this moment, everything you hear, everything you feel, all knowledge about distant galaxies and the extraordinary worlds that exist within atoms and molecules and cells, imagine that all of that is what you are. Not as an abstract understanding, but as something that you understand deeply — that you own it, that you are One with everything that is. And as such, all of it simply *is*, without judgment. That kind of expansive thought is what provides you with the ability to sit in your Soul every moment, deeply connected and capable of witnessing all that is and knowing it to be who you are.

Take this moment, breathe deeply, and let all of these words ebb away and return to that simple peace of sitting deep within your Soul. You are now ready to begin the process of getting unstuck.

Getting Unstuck

Habitual thought is creative thought.

— *Solano*

You exist in a realm where all thoughts have the potential for manifestation. It is that potential that constitutes the Fields of Plenty. If plenty for you is plenty of peace, love, abundance, creativity and joy, your thoughts are consistently directed toward what you want rather than what you do not want. But for many that is not the case.

Repeated or habitual thought creates what manifests around you. If you dwell on poverty or abandonment or disease and illness or any number of things that do not match the Soul's understanding of the eternal and abundant nature of life, you are dwelling on what you do not desire to create.

Early on when you incarnated, you felt the beating of your heart, you experienced your lungs rhythmically taking in air and releasing it. You felt the rhythms of the Earth — light and dark, and the celestial impact of the seasons. You experienced the habits and patterns of a household, your body's patterns of hunger, of need, of fullness and elimination.

Your driving need was to understand and control your experience. The repetition and habits of human life and the desire to understand and control them is the genesis of what ultimately became your habitual thought.

Over time you began to understand a few things. You associated those things with language. You noticed that if you spoke certain words, there were certain results, and it became relatively consistent. And that consistency was something that gave you a sense of success, a sense of control.

But then you encountered moments when you experienced trauma. Perhaps a parent misunderstood you. So instead of being fed or cleansed or your needs being met, instead of being supported and loved through a fear, what you experienced instead was judgment or criticism or worse, and in such a moment confusion reigned. The developing brain laid down a deeper circuitry in the central nervous system based on the need for survival. You judged that particular event and began to expect it, in some instances developing a hyper vigilance about it.

It is in such moments that habitual thought goes awry. Such moments are the basic building blocks of the altered ego — the aspect of you that takes on the values and judgments of your society, family, and tribe, and imposes them critically, and usually inconsistently, upon you. At its best the altered ego's function is to understand and skillfully maneuver this dream in which you are dwelling. Its job is to protect and defend your body, your creation. But the desire to protect your body is often more compelling than the need to understand and move creatively and gracefully through the traumatic event. This reoccurs throughout your life and results in the patterns that become your habitual thought.

It is important to understand this rudimentary pattern so that you can develop tools with which to transform it. The goal is to steer habitual thought toward what you want to create in your life, rather than what you do not want in your life.

Every moment you have an opportunity to
build new habitual thought.

— Solano

THE ELECTROMAGNETIC FIELD

Individuals around you who had already identified with their altered ego reinforced the development of your altered ego. Perhaps your mother was in a constant state of anxiety, or your father was an alcoholic. Maybe your sister was afraid of being alone. The emotions that exist within a household create a prevailing vibratory frequency. As a child you were very susceptible to the frequencies of others because you were trying to learn and understand. You were absorbing everything and seeking to establish rapport. Being surrounded by the energy of others who are identified with their altered ego often translates into a familiar tone in the child's body and that familiarity also provides a significant basis of your own habitual thoughts.

This happened while you were gathering skills of language. You began to assign language to your emotions; to your body and the way it felt, to what you longed for, what your body needed — food, warmth, touch.

> *Electromagnetic frequency — The*
> *electromagnetic field that surrounds a human*
> *body.*

As you were building language and studying others around you, you began to take on their habits — not just their external habits, but also their *electromagnetic frequency.* You did not just mimic outer behavior; you mimicked their tone as well. You did this because the people around you lived what you thought to be success-ful lives, even if they were not what you would consider to be successful lives now. They were adults. They could get food. They could move about on their own. They had things that you wanted. They held the keys to your freedom. So you began to assimilate their ways, their habits, even the way that they lived in their body, the way they walked, the way they held themselves, the way that they interacted with others. You were studying and assimilating everything about them.

Ultimately you departed from that process to your own discovery and exploration, but not until after a frequency was set up as familiar, your unique frequency modified by the prevailing frequencies around you, translated into emotion. Then as you gained language skills you began to talk about your emotions and the physical states of the body, and you began to affirm those states as your beliefs about the nature of life in a body.

Beliefs are a key element of habitual thought. Beliefs are generated to explain life to you. Do you believe that you are forever? Do you believe that you are abundant

and that the universe is an abundant place? Do you
believe that you are worthy of love and health and joy and
fulfillment? Do you believe that you have the resources
to experience that and sustain it? Your consistent efforts
to upgrade the habitual beliefs of your family of origin
have the potential to result in beliefs of immortality,
abundance, and a loving, supportive Universe filled with
joy and fulfillment, but not without conscious effort to
that end.

If due to fear, disappointment, loss, or abandonment you
have developed habitually contracted thought patterns,
you can do something about it. Every moment is another
opportunity to create a new habitual thought pattern just
as every breath is another opportunity to take in fresh air.
This very moment you can engage thoughts that allow
you to feel expansive, that you feel empowered by, that
contribute to a more expansive electromagnetic field, and
that provide the ability to overcome the habitual thought
processes that have previously lead to the same result.

Establish an observer to gain access to
your Soul's perspective.
— *Solano*

THE OBSERVER

Love. Non-judgment. Knowing. Integrity. Truth. These are examples of the Soul's values. Inhabiting your Soul's values allows you to live your life supple, expansive, and open, because you dwell closer to your original, unaltered state. Living as such promotes sustainable habitual thought.

The values of the altered ego are constrictive values: anger, deceit, closed-mindedness, judgment, possessiveness, fear, and identification with the body. If you find yourself habitually engaged in such values, then it becomes important to identify the habitual thoughts that result in such values, and to interrupt them. You do this by bringing conscious attention to the patterns. Instead of identifying with them, you take a step back, acknowledge that they are thoughts born of the limited mind's time-based perspective, and affirm that you are your immortal Soul.

Think about the fear of aging. Those who fear aging habitually think: "I am getting old." They think they are simply being truthful with themselves. But is such a thought aligned with the Soul's values, or is it aligned with the altered ego's values? There is a simple test: if you feel lifted and expansive thinking a thought, you are identified with your Soul. If you feel contracted or fearful when you think it, you are identified with the altered ego. Most are fearful about the prospect of aging — fearful that their body will betray them, fearful that they will be weakened or abandoned or unwanted by society.

To transform a habitual thought like that, you must first establish an *observer* of your thought processes to notice that you are thinking the thought. Next, find a thought that will be the perfect antidote. For example, "I am forever, vital and essential to the Universe" or "My body is composed of light. I identify with the Light that I am and that light renews my body every moment."

> *To establish an observer, simply imagine that you are at a console and in front of you is a stage. Imagine that everything you think and hear and feel is displayed in front of you in words, sounds, or images. And you, the observer, have control. You can stop your thoughts, slow them down, reverse them, or simply observe them.*

Consider some other habitual thoughts — fear of being poor, fear of disease, fear of violence or mishap. With each of these, first observe yourself in the act of thinking the thought that is not aligned with your Soul's values. Then counteract that with a thought that is the expansive version of that thought — "I am radiant consciousness with all the resources necessary for robust health. I am guided surely and protected always by my Soul."

At Solano's direction I learned to establish my observer
through meditation. I started meditating regularly when
I was in my twenties, but still I sometimes find myself
overcome by thoughts that get out of hand and interrupt
my efforts. In such moments, I have to tell my altered ego
to stop... to just stop. Then I take a deep breath and
I imagine myself in a watchful place, observing my
thoughts and behavior. From there, my thoughts quiet,
my problems diminish, and my level of compassion
increases. This is my observer.

If I find myself in an emotional cycle that has been set up
by the altered ego's fears, I also find that it's really helpful
if I do something that demands so much of me that I can
no longer stay in my linear (altered ego) thought process.
Yoga is very helpful in such moments because of the
physical focus that is required and especially because of
the transformational effect of ujjayi breath. Sometimes,
if a yoga class is not available to me I will simply do ujjayi
pranayama. I can do this if I'm driving, if I am wakeful in
the middle of the night, in the midst of a crowd, walking,
biking, doing chores. I find it immensely transformational

when I find myself stuck with an emotion that has been prompted by the altered ego.

If you are unfamiliar with ujjayi breath, it is a very simple practice. Slightly restrict your vocal chords as you are breathing so that you begin to hear an audible sound like the wind through the trees. In the beginning I suggest that you count, seven seconds on the inhale and match that on the exhale. The longer and slower the breath, the more the emotional tone of your body will change. This practice is very effective for helping to neutralize adrenaline that may be coursing through your system.

Illness, too, exists in the realm of Infinite Intelligence.

— *Solano*

Take a moment to consider the habitual thoughts that trouble you. Do you fear illness? Fear is an unconscious affirmation. If your Soul's curriculum has designed for you to learn about illness and all the lessons that it brings, if your emotions and the frequency they set up in your light field align with your genetics and environmental influences, then the sum total of all of those elements becomes your destiny and you experience illness.

However, if you affirm that you are healthy and vital in thought and deed, if your Soul's curriculum does not require illness for the wisdom that it seeks, you will likely know good health. If you bless your food, your body, the technology you interact with, and bless your environment — such things as pollen and sunshine — the act of blessing acknowledges the Divine spark in everything. Acknowledging that what *is* is manifested precisely in alignment with your Soul's journey helps you maintain a relationship to your manifested reality that sustains good health.

What does a Soul have to gain by the physical body experiencing disease? Surely, wisdom can be achieved without going through the hardship of debilitating disease.

A Soul may choose to manifest a physical challenge for any of a myriad of reasons — to learn humility or compassion, to understand the value of patience — but always, overarching all of those reasons is the primary directive for human incarnation on Earth — to gain the wisdom that comes from migrating from identity as singular to an identity of being One with Infinite Wisdom.

Illness has a clarifying effect on an individual, resulting in a reordering of priorities. How often have you heard of someone having a physical crisis and returning to health resolved to live life in a different manner? This can manifest in dedicating their attentions to improving their lifestyle, their environment, or their habits. Many come back to health more focused and determined to live more simply, often with a newfound emphasis on service.

There are also those instances where illness in an individual serves a system — a family or a community — bringing awareness or prompting cohesion, forgiveness, and evolution. An ill child can bring a family much deeper into relationship, spurred into changes that would not have been prompted otherwise. There is also societal illness and the impact that it has. Plagues and their role in the evolution of human consciousness cannot be overlooked. There is no dispute to the many effects the Black Plague had on Europe in the Middle Ages. With the sudden depopulation of the continent, vast fortunes changed hands and communal relationships were altered, laying the groundwork for the end of serfdom and the start of the Renaissance.

Currently, the HIV/AIDS epidemic has global ramifications. In the Westernized world it has played an important part in the growing visibility of the LGBT community. It has resulted in the redistribution of wealth and has played a significant role in the polarization of the political climate, particularly in the United States. Elsewhere in the world it has drawn greater attention to the effects of poverty and the inequality of women, the vulnerability of children in impoverished communities, and ultimately will result in massive changes in Africa, India, and China.

Illness, disease, and physical handicaps do not dwell outside the realm of the Infinite Intelligence. It is ever more crucial in light of illness, particularly life-threatening illness, to establish the observer and to remember the immortality of the Soul. Willfully seek to know what wisdom the Soul desires to gain from any physical challenge and to embrace it as a benevolent force for change.

It is consistency that establishes a new pattern of thought.

— *Solano*

When you've established an observer, and you notice
yourself engaged in habitual thought that affirms what
you do not want, when you have interrupted that thought
and you have created another thought to counteract that
habitual thought, the next step is to be consistent. Rather
than succumbing to the frailty of fear or the altered ego's
insistence that you are growing old or that you are ill
or that you do not have enough money, use your will to
establish healthier patterns of habitual thought.

Breaking Habitual Thought
- *Establish an observer to identify when a habitual thought occurs.*
- *Create a thought of a higher frequency to counteract the habit.*
- *Be consistent.*
- *Engage the will to establish a new habitual thought.*

You are responsible for the vitality of your will.

— *Solano*

WILL

Will is your birthright. It is the ability to decide upon and
initiate action. Will fuels your creativity. It is the key to
your destiny. There may be times in your life when your
will feels depleted. Sometimes the vicissitudes of life
drain from the body the verve and passion for life that
connects you to your will. But the will can be resurrected.
By retreating within, drawing yourself down into the purity
of your Soul's values, and remaining there for a time, you
can reconnect with your will.

Fasting and turning inward to seek silence are helpful
practices when habitual thought that is not aligned with
the Soul's values takes root in your life. You leak vital life
force when habitual thought results in behaviors that
reinforce those very same habitual thoughts. This is the
basis of feeling stuck, and when you feel stuck, you leak
energy that causes a diminishment of vitality in the body.
The Soul does not lose power. Rather, the vitality that the
Soul provides to the body is frittered away as a result of
habitual thought that does not acknowledge that you are
forever and eternally supported.

When you leak vital life force, it diminishes the sense that renewal is possible, that you are capable of new thought processes. If you succumb to that gravity, then you become rigid, frail, contracted, and fearful. On the other hand, if you use your will to renew yourself with expansive thought, then habits which have a tendency to exaggerate with maturity are neutralized and what replaces them is a character that is joyful. You then possess an uplifted consciousness that can inspire others through its clarity and coherent frequency.

Bringing yourself back to a place of stillness, especially through daily meditation, renews your will. This then provides you with the ability to have a thought process that is connected to what you want your life to be, rather than what you do not want it to be.

You are responsible for what you think. As you accept that responsibility, you gain the ability to steer your life with greater precision in the language of your thoughts. Then your will can guide you in the effort to design a garden of thoughts that completely supports you.

*When I first met Shelly she was in the depths of grief
over the break up of a relationship. She had moved to the
Northwest, leaving a good job as a set designer because
she had fallen in love. The prospect of a relationship
proved to be more compelling to her than the relative
security of her job. So she uprooted herself and moved.*

*She was living hand to mouth and drinking too much
alcohol. This talented woman found herself in a very dark
place, wondering how to get out of it.*

*In listening to her story I heard her say such things as,
"I knew it was a bad decision, I knew he was unstable, I
knew he wasn't the marrying type, etc." When I asked her
why she would knowingly make a bad decision, she said,
"I wanted a relationship so badly, I was willing to take a
chance."*

*In one session we started talking about what she wanted
out of life. Every desire she expressed about relationship,
fulfilling work, or where she wanted to live, in the next
breath she would negate and tell me why it couldn't be,
wouldn't be.*

I pointed out how she was undermining herself, affirming what she did not want instead of accepting what she had created. We went through an exercise to imagine the emotional response of living her ideal life. Not just seeing the pictures in her mind, but feeling the emotions.

We went through each element in her life, one by one, and I had her write down what she wanted, specifically. We went through the kind of relationship she wanted (loving, tender, creative, passionate, committed), the kind of lifestyle she wanted (to live on the water, community of good friends close by, travel for work and play, recognition for her accomplishments, impart her knowledge to others), economic situation (out of debt, good salary, occasional extra gigs), health (lose weight, build strength, cut out the booze). She took the time to embrace what each of these results, brought into the present, would feel like in her life.

Within the week of writing down what she wanted, she was offered a job at a high-end specialty construction company running a crew doing installations of very complex and highly artistic architectural features of public buildings and expensive homes. Within two weeks she'd been offered a live-aboard houseboat in a community of people who became her good friends and extended community. Within three months she met a man with whom she shared many creative sensibilities. They fell in love and created a home together.

It may seem that I'm heading toward the closing line of a fairy tale ending. But rather than "living happily ever after" I would say she is constantly on that knife's edge of creating the life she wants as opposed to the life that she does not want.

Getting unstuck requires consistent creativity focused on what one wants and generating the electromagnetic frequency that matches.

Every choice serves the Soul's drive toward being
completely One with the Divine.

— *Solano*

THE SOUL'S GYROSCOPE

Sometimes an individual is drawn to a habitual dream of incarnating on Earth, or to a particular bloodline. Some become habituated to the quest for power, or the quest to understand gender identity. But what is important to recognize in such a habit is that the Soul would not agree with any habituation if it did not serve its drive toward becoming wholly and completely One with the Divine. The Soul has patience born of immortality.

You have free choice, free will. You can choose a reality over and over again. It is so in your journey on the Earth, lifetime after lifetime — and it is so in an individual life. You can continue to habituate to a particular drive, or addiction, or fear, or shortcoming. But the Soul has a gyroscopic guidance system. If you, identified with your

altered ego, are knocked off balance, because of being compelled by habit, the Soul takes that blow and uses it to steer you to what you need to know about that gap in your understanding of being One with God.

Your evolution does not happen in a vacuum,
it happens within the consciousness
that permeates all and therefore affects all.
— *Solano*

The Soul's gyroscopic guidance carries you along on your arc of experience with its goal of reuniting with the One. When you arrive there you arrive completely informed that you are one with the Divine.

Embracing the knowledge that you are a Soul that is forever is not an invitation to passivity about your growth and your reach for consciousness. Nor is the knowledge that the Earth and other individuals are immortal an invitation to become passive about the conditions on Earth or the need for change or healing.

Passivity is not a value aligned with the Soul — peace is, surrender is, non-judgment is, but not passivity. Conditions like hunger and violence and environmental degradation are circumstances that call for you to align with your Soul's values and to remember that you are here with an aim and a purpose. You would not be on this journey if you did not desire to learn from and be a force on the Earth, one that embodies what it is to become more fully aligned with the Soul's values. Greed, possessiveness, and competition are neutralized when you inhabit the Soul's values.

The creation of your own utopia, in which you are filled with love, joy, creativity, openness, non-judgment, compassion, and generosity, is the means to most effectively change the consciousness of greed or violence or judgment in your society. Ultimately such creativity prompts evolution. But you, living a Soulful life, become the gyroscopic element that helps to design where that creativity leads. It may lead to changes in the habitual thought of the group. It may lead to changes in laws or consciousness. Your growth affects the consciousness of the whole.

Remember every moment you are here to become God.

— *Solano*

You are consciousness itself. You are God. Every moment you dwell in Fields of Plenty. Remember that this life is simply a dream in which you are learning to move from state of consciousness to state of consciousness. You continue on beyond this physical reality. Remind yourself why you are here, why you do it, why you breathe, why you think, why you engage this entertainment.

If you remind yourself that it is for your growth, that it is to become one with the Divine Consciousness, and if you become relentless about becoming conscious, then you can achieve what it is that you've incarnated to achieve.

Anchoring Hope

The time has come to be
more precise in your growth process.

— *Solano*

When considering the Fields of Plenty, it is natural to think about what you want to manifest in this three-dimensional reality. Most often you imagine a goal and then begin to hope for it to manifest. This is largely an unconscious process.

The means to manifest anything begins with using the imagination to create the emotion, present tense, which is associated with the desired experience. "Hoping" for an imagined outcome affirms that it is not present, but rather dwells in the un-manifested "future." It creates a mixed emotion that affects the electromagnetic field around your body. Your electromagnetic field is the field of influence that then manifests your experience. When you hope for something, what is created time and again is simply the experience of hoping, not the experience of fulfillment.

It is important to know what you are hoping for, and what the emotional state of hope generates in your body and in your electromagnetic field. Then you must eliminate the time and space that you believe separates the present moment from the "hoped for" outcome.

In ancient Hebrew there was no tense associated with future. You spoke of the future in context, but when one made prophecies about what was coming or what was desired, the prophesy was spoken in the present tense, as though in the imagination of the speaker that event had already happened. It had been felt. It had been heard. It had been seen. It was spoken as the *prophetic present*. You inhabit the prophetic present when you are living in the now. When you live in the now you are seated in your Soul and its infinite wisdom.

Much of this linguistic style was lost when the Jewish tribe was taken into captivity in Babylon, where they adopted Aramaic, but still Hebrew remained a living language, sustained as such within the texts of those who protected that body of knowledge. Even in the living Hebrew language of today, future and past are conveyed contextually. There is much to learn from this example, because most languages, English for example, only allow you to speak of the future as a thing that does not yet exist — something for which one hopes or longs or wishes.

When you intend to speak truthfully, you use the future tense to speak of something that may happen someday, in the future. That sets the proclaimed future experience on the perimeter of your light field. You relate to it as something distant. For most individuals the experience is imagined literally up and forward a little distance from the body as though it is something that one is moving toward. It is not placed in one's Soul. Not held as "I have seen this, I have heard this, it is done. I experience it as being so."

Words have power.

— *Solano*

THE DEFAULT EMOTIONAL RESPONSE

Sometimes you will speak an affirmation or proclamation with no apparent change. In such instances, the internal dialogue you are having about your "reality" is actually affirming something different than the affirmation or proclamation. A negative affirmation such as "I am getting old" can become a default emotional response triggered, for example, simply by looking in the mirror or feeling a chronic pain. This happens when a habit has developed of feeling that pain or looking at that body image and talking about it negatively. The default emotional response then becomes a kind of shorthand with no conscious affirming thought, just a spontaneous emotion in response to looking in the mirror. In such a case an affirmation such as "I am filled with infinite energy and joy" may be negated by the spontaneous emotional affirmations you are making when you look in the mirror or looking at your body.

This requires concerted attention to the default emotional response. You do this by recognizing that it is the altered ego that built the negative association, set it up that the observer will alert you when you are about to engage the default emotional response (or interrupt it if it has already begun). Step back from the habitual emotional response. Observe how it strikes a familiar tone in your body. Trace it back to the judgment or fear and observe how the thought became an unconscious emotional response. Then choose a new, expansive, and neutralizing thought. Making this new thought habitual takes repetition. Consider how many repetitions it took to build the default emotional response and be patient, but determined, with yourself as you build a new, more expansive habit.

Your body does not distinguish between a fully
articulated "fantasy" and so-called "reality."
— *Solano*

In sports psychology, some coaches urge their athletes to use their imagination to see, feel, smell, taste the experience of the accomplishment, the triumph that they want. Your body, as you know from your experiences of fear and lust and hunger and fulfillment, will generate emotional states in response to your imagination by affecting the hormones that course through your body.

It is possible to apply this in your life. You can use your imagination to bring the completion that you want into the prophetic present. This then creates an emotional state that affects the chemical makeup of your body. You then create a state of reality that is manifested in direct response to the changes in the frequency of your light field — your field of influence. This is something that you have done, mostly unconsciously, all of your life, with both negative and positive outcomes.

Creating the Prophetic Present

Take a moment and write down things for which you have been hoping. Then write down each of those hoped-for experiences in a statement that is in the present tense.

> *"I hope I will be accepted into that college"*
> *becomes "I have been accepted into that*
> *college, I know what it feels like, looks like,*
> *smells like. It is done. I have experienced it."*

Remember that in the prophetic present what is hoped for has already been seen, heard, understood, felt and experienced. It is done. It is completed. The reason for writing them down as present tense reality is so you can begin to identify how often your inner dialogue is a conversation about the hoped-for experience in the future tense, which you have now written in the prophetic present.

Once you have done this for each of your desired outcomes, establish an observer to note when the altered ego begins to hope for something out of the moment. Then affirm each time that the hoped-for experience is now and, therefore, use your creativity to generate the emotion of fulfillment.

Inhabiting the prophetic present
you neutralize negative association.

— *Solano*

NEGATIVE ASSOCIATION

When you do not create the emotion of fulfillment, but instead generate an emotion that counteracts pure desire, you are building a negative association. For example, when an individual on a limited budget desires something, and they see someone who can afford that item, they sometimes experience envy or jealousy or judgment. This creates a negative emotional association to the desire.

Negative associations cause you to leak energy. They block your creative power. You then miss the opportunity to create through imagination an emotion that is aligned with the frequency of fulfillment.

Negative associations must be identified and neutralized in order for you to consciously inhabit the Fields of Plenty. The relationship between you and the desired end — the experience of abundance, good health, and successful relationships — must be simple and direct without side trips into negative association.

Put simply, ease of manifestation requires anchoring hope as a present tense experience of the desired fulfillment and neutralizing any negative association that arises surrounding your desires.

EXERCISE TO IDENTIFY
NEGATIVE ASSOCIATIONS

Ask yourself what you dream of creating in your life. What is your definition of dwelling in Fields of Plenty? Write it all down.

(Example) I desire....

- *Plenty such that I can travel in complete comfort anytime I wish wherever I wish without a thought to the cost.*

- *Abundance such that I can live surrounded by beauty. My home is my canvas for creative expression. Any idea I have for beauty, comfort, delight, and artistic expression I have the ability to make it so — hire craftsmen, talent, artists, buy the materials and live comfortably and elegantly every moment of my existence.*

- *Wealth such that I can have a creative idea and hire the team to execute the idea — guiding as I choose due to my position as financier.*

- *Abundance such that I can help others achieve their dreams by empowering, mentoring, teaching, sharing my experience and knowledge and my resources.*

- *Wealth such that all bodily care, maintenance, support and improvement is available without concern for expense.*

- *Abundance in the form of confidence, ease, peace and satisfaction on every level — mental (constant improvement through learning), spiritual (deep understanding that abundance comes from the Infinite Potential), and physical (comfort, ease, sensual delight and satisfaction).*

- *Wealth such that all support is available without concern for expense — accountant, bookkeeper, housecleaner, gardener, assistants, editors, lawyers, chefs, drivers, pilots, masseurs, doctors, teachers, coaches, technical assistants, web designers, researchers, painters, every kind of support imaginable.*

- *Ease such that I can surround myself with loved ones, children, animals, and family, and the ability to support each appropriate to their needs.*

1. *Now focus on any one of the things that you identified as part of your experience of dwelling in Fields of Plenty. Let's say it's freedom and the first thing you do when you think of achieving freedom is you think "to be free I have to have money or the kids have to be on their own" or "I'll be free after my father dies" or any number of things that stop you from simply sitting in the frequency of freedom, this moment. Those are negative associations.*

2. *Stop at the first negative association. Say to yourself,
"I am free. NOW, this moment. I know freedom in every
fiber of my body. It is done. It is mine. I now generate, in
the electromagnetic field that surrounds my body, the
frequency of complete and utter freedom. It is so."*

3. *Then live with that as your internally generated "reality"
daily. Affirm it. Pierce the illusion that you have generated
around you as your "life." Remember that you created
that dream, you have prophesied your life. Now begin to
prophesy the life that you desire. Be as intentional and
consistent about creating freedom as you have been
about creating your current circumstances.*

*You don't have to approach it as work. Approach it rather
as a child would or an artist would — imagine that you
are free and feel it. Picture yourself (or if you don't easily
generate pictures in your mind's eye, then feel yourself)
living your life as one who is free in every way.*

*Occasionally, a negative association will crop up again
— "To achieve such and such, I need money, I need to be
healthier, I need courage, I need to be younger." Those are
negative associations because they take you away from
the simple straight line to fulfillment that comes from
generating the emotion, the frequency of the thing or
experience that you desire.*

*This is how you create your life — the dream of your life.
You'll find it more fulfilling to intentionally create what
you want than to create by default by letting negative
association hijack your process.*

By engaging a hoped-for experience as a
present-tense consciousness, hope transforms into
fulfillment in your body.
— *Solano*

It is important to determine whether your hopes are aligned with the Soul's values. The simple test is this: If a desire grows out of a sense of lack or fear, it is born of an altered ego value. From the altered ego's perspective you are singularly alone and all else is the "other." If what you want is based in the joy of creativity and love of life — that is a Soul value and the Soul's values will ultimately prevail.

You are immortal — a Soul dwelling in a body. The altered ego with its limited beliefs and longings will die and it knows it. That is one of the reasons that there is breath-lessness and strain that is associated with the altered ego's hopes and dreams.

As you scan those things that you long to achieve in your life, hold them up against the Soul's values to determine if your dreams are in alignment with your Soul's curriculum. This will bring you into deeper wisdom and assist you in the process of dwelling in the present.

The Soul's curriculum governs what manifests in your life.
— *Solano*

Rebecca was a beautiful, talented, and warm-hearted woman who came to me periodically for counseling. She had very ambitious dreams for her life. She wanted to be a successful recording artist, she wanted to marry and have a family. To that end she moved to Los Angeles and set about pursuing her career.

In college, she'd had a relationship with the scion of a wealthy family. He was intelligent and talented, but he had extreme mood swings that sometimes resulted in him being emotionally or physically abusive to her. It was a bitter day when she realized that she could no longer be with him and she grieved having to break off the engagement and the loss of the dream of being married to him.

This experience resulted in a negative emotional association to intimate relationships and it colored much of her subsequent experience.

Decades passed and she did not have another significant relationship. Nevertheless, she continued to dream of having a husband and a family. What she hadn't noticed was that whenever she would access that dream, at the *very same moment she would access the negative emotions she had with her former fiancé. This came to her awareness as we talked.*

She continued to pursue her dreams of being a recording artist. She put together a band and made an album. Opportunities came to her — one in particular appeared to be a big break; she was to go on tour and open for a famous recording artist. Though she agreed contractually to not leak the news about this gig until given the green light, she didn't think it would matter and went ahead and announced to her fan base. The headliner's management team then fired her. Her disappointment was deep and she went through another bout of grief over this seeming failure. As a result she built more negative associations, this time to opportunities to advance her career.

Small gigs came here and there, singing backup for friends on their albums, gigging at parties and expos. The album didn't have the intended result of her being signed by a label, nor did a manager step up to represent her.

The years began to add up and Rebecca still hoped for a baby. She wanted to see her own flesh and blood... to nurture it and hold it, to present her beloved mother with a grandchild. It was a deep and abiding drive. Friends suggested that she just get pregnant, not wait for the perfect guy. But she held onto her hopes and dreams. First, there would be artistic success, then monetary success, then the guy, and then the family. It's how she wanted it. How she felt it had to be.

The problem was that as the decades went by the negative associations began to take a toll. A guy would appear and soon thereafter disappear because of her negative associations and because she had not updated her dreams. Rather than set new goals and perhaps begin a new career, she would collect unemployment or take a temporary job to make ends meet.

Then she stopped menstruating. The dream of having her own child moved out of the realm of possibility. She tried for a while to imagine marrying and adopting, but still, no man appeared on the horizon.

The last time I saw her, Rebecca was in her sixties. She was living in a rented room and she was trying to sell her library of songs. She was still single and had no children. Despite that, she was radiantly happy and quite lucid when she told me that she had had a profound epiphany that her life had really been about breaking the "habit" of procreating and that because she had not had children, she was able to more clearly understand her life as a Soul on a journey.

The sense I got from her was that she felt far richer than she would have had she married and taken a path that she had walked lifetime after lifetime. Think, for instance, of a nun who takes an intentional vow of poverty, chastity, and service — the aim of such a life is to be in closer communion with "God." I make no distinction here. Rebecca's life was very much like the life of a nun without the abbey or the cloister or the organized religion. For her, Fields of Plenty came in the form of a deeper and self-inspired relationship with the Divine — through observation and contemplation.

You know what you have come here to learn.

— *Solano*

Ask yourself what you want to achieve in your life. Are those desires still pertinent? Do your desires match your Soul's values? The test is simple. Ask yourself this: "If I knew in every fiber of my being that I am forever and One with the Divine Source, is this goal what I would want to draw into my prophetic present?"

You know, in that deep, still place in your being, what it is that your most elevated, most conscious, most awake self wants to experience here on Earth. If that dream of being fabulously wealthy, or the dream of finding your perfect mate or the dream of being a recording star is prompted by lack or emptiness or fear or insecurity — you know when you are completely honest with yourself if this is so. If a dream is funded by the altered ego's search for safety, then that dream is likely to provide you with a circuitous route to the fulfillment of the Soul's curriculum.

If what you hope for is something so pervasive that even if you felt completely fulfilled in this moment you would still call it into the prophetic present — then it is undoubtedly something that is part of your Soul's curriculum.

If it is not aligned with the Soul's values, given this test, then take it off of your list. This is part of the process of dwelling in the prophetic present. Being up to date. Being current in your body. Releasing any desires that no longer pertain to your current self. Leftover goals that have not been released create neuroses and addictions because of negative emotional associations.

Cleaning up the list of things that you desire in this life-time will diminish the static generated by leftover dreams. Then when you do assign value to an experience enough to draw it into the prophetic present, to proclaim and to acknowledge it as done, it is accomplished simply and with grace.

*Arthur was in his fifties when he came to me to do
some work on specific issues. He was successful, had no
troublesome addictions, and was in a healthy long-term
relationship, but he had begun to feel that he had veered
off course in his life and wanted to go back and pick up
a stitch. In our first session, he told me about a spiritual
teacher that he had gotten involved with when he was in
his twenties. The teacher was very charismatic and tended
to be very provocative with his followers. It wasn't unusual
for people to leave their families or their careers and make
dramatic lifestyle changes. Often they would move across
the country to be near the teacher.*

*When he met the teacher, Arthur was studying opera in
New York City. He showed great promise and, moreover,
loved what he was doing. But one day his spiritual teacher
was doing a seminar and the schedule conflicted with
Arthur's acting class, so Arthur told the teacher that he
wasn't going to be able to attend the seminar. The teacher
fixed Arthur with his piercing eyes and said, "You don't
need that class — you already know everything you need to
know about acting." As Arthur related this to me in session,*

it was apparent that it was a very pivotal moment in his life. He told me that in that moment he chose to attend the seminar, immediately stopped taking acting classes, and within six months, moved away from New York City to be near his teacher.

Not long after he moved, Arthur became aware that the teacher had created a financial investment scheme and was encouraging his followers to participate, regardless of their ability to afford the risk. It seemed like a scam to Arthur. At the same time, Arthur learned that his teacher had taken a younger mistress and was leaving his wife. Arthur couldn't reconcile what he felt were lapses of integrity in the master, whom he had come to respect and even worship.

What troubled him most at this point in his life were the "what ifs." What if he'd remained in New York City? What if he hadn't abandoned his career? Who would he be? Would he have achieved more? Would he have fulfilled his dream of becoming an opera singer?

In our sessions together, we examined the choices he had made using a very simple guideline: Given what you knew and the things that you felt most passionately about, could you have made different choices at the time? In every instance, the answer was that he had made the choice he made because he felt compelled to it.

This was part of a larger process of getting up to date, like deleting old unused programs in a computer. If a program is running in the background on a computer but isn't actively used or providing service, it is using up energy and slowing down the computer. It was an apt analogy for the circumstances in Arthur's life.

Ultimately, what he came to realize was that if opera was his first priority — his Soul's urging — he would have continued to sing, no matter what. But his greatest drive and passion had been about personal discovery, especially discovery about his spiritual life, his Soul. Hence the decision to overturn his career plans and follow a spiritual teacher. Yes, he experienced disillusionment with the teacher, but he didn't choose to go back to New York City. He concluded that by following his passion he was following his Soul's curriculum. The questioning at this point in his life was due to the need to bring the altered ego up to date instead of having it running an old program and generating emotions of incompletion or, even less desirable, failure.

When faith becomes knowing,
then do you dwell in Fields of Plenty.
— *Solano*

THE SOURCE OF KNOWING

Faith is another aspect of hope. Faith in another human being, faith in another source of power outside of you, faith in a higher good, faith in a more intelligent source than you — is misplaced. When, instead of faith, you come to the realization that you are the same infinite intelligence that has created all that is, faith becomes knowing. When you dwell in knowing you are dwelling at the source of your own power and the infinite resources of the universe.

Faith, like hope, gives power to the illusion of time. When you incarnate here you agree to the illusion of time. It entertains you, the notion that you are a child and that you grow up and gain certain privileges and skills. Just as it is entertaining for you to go into your dreams when you are asleep and enter a whole new world. You have a body there and experiences there that generate emotions. Sometimes what you do there seems to span a great amount of time, but then you waken and you've only been asleep for a few moments. This entire lifetime will seem the same, when you waken from the dream of this three-dimensional realm.

In this dream you are slowed down so you can experience states of consciousness incrementally, evolving toward the inevitability of the altered ego and the body having to be surrendered. It is most important to understand that the life that is true is the life of your energy that is immortal. This is what you experience when you settle into the radiance of your Soul. In that experience you are One with the Divine. Therein you are imminently and expansively wise with access to any and all creativity.

Dwelling in the knowledge of the Soul's *foreverness* provides you with the ability to migrate from having faith in something outside of you to knowing that you are the source of your experience. It allows you to move from hope to accomplishment. The fortune that you want to amass, that relationship that you want to have, the body that you want to heal, that song that you want to sing, the film that you want to direct — the fulfillment of those dreams comes not from migrating outward, but from settling into the place within where all is known, accomplished, and fulfilled this moment.

Clearing the body of emotional residue
makes it easier to dwell in the moment.
— *Solano*

The thought that all is fulfilled this moment often causes anxiety for the altered ego. The altered ego clings to the dream of this world where manifestation is slowed down, and where there are accomplishments that you build brick by brick. Of course, you may live your life this way. It is important that you understand that you are doing so by choice. All of the things that you seek you do so because you know you will grow wise as a result of the experience. It is the experience that prompts the migration from altered ego identification to identification with your Soul.

When you find yourself experiencing a negative emotion because you were thwarted in an endeavor, recognize that you generate the negative emotion because you are identified with the altered ego, instead of being identified with the Soul.

To live fully in the prophetic present, the body must resonate with what you are generating in your imagination. If trying to imagine the experience of abundance, you go around and around with all of the reasons that abundance cannot be — your age or lack of education or the economy, all of the things that the altered ego identifies as handicaps — those handicaps become just that.

If the body does not have a clear resonance, it is because your imagination has been actively engaged in creating a conflicting circuitry. Do not blame your body. Your body is the residue of your thoughts and the emotional processes that are sparked by your thoughts. That is what determines the frequency that you inhabit. The goal is to be able to move from a state of consciousness in which there are negative associations or blockages that prevent you from accessing the prophetic present, to a state of consciousness in which you can dream your life the way that you want it.

Embracing What Is

You have prophesied the life that you are now living.

— *Solano*

Accepting the life that you have created allows you to address the blockages in your energy field that prevent you from creating the life that you want. Energetic blockages occur when tension has settled in your energy meridians from former disappointments, or fears, or in some cases acculturation from others or from learned blockages from your family of origin.

To clear blockages in the body you must first understand that the blockages were created by the altered ego's judgment of your experience here on this planet. Fully embracing the dream that you are dreaming, exactly as it is, allows you to stop creating more tension in the process of trying to change an aspect of your dream. Sometimes you work so hard to accomplish a task, putting all your strength and energy into it and getting more and more tense in the process. When you stop and release the tension and then return to the task, it seems easier. It flows. This is one of the benefits of embracing what *is* in your life.

These log jams are not necessarily at points associated with your central nervous system, but rather are in the pathways of energy that were identified in the deep meditations of ancient Chinese healers and have been

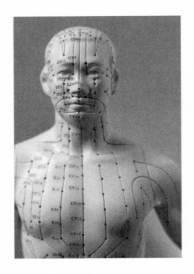

confirmed through many generations of empirical exploration by acupuncturists and *qi gong* practitioners. Osteopaths also use knowledge of this energy system.

If you are stretching your legs and you find that there is pain in your left hip, what you know is that you need to release muscle tension in order to move through the pain. So you breathe into it. You then pull back from it a bit as you are breathing in and then as you are exhaling, you move into it again. The process of clearing energetic blockages is similar in that you direct awareness to a place in your body where there is tension of an energetic nature, and then you press into it and breathe. Then you pull back a little and as you exhale you move deeper into it, releasing tension with each exhale.

EXERCISE TO DISSOLVE BLOCKAGES IN THE BODY

Lie down, supine, where you are most comfortable.
Think of something that you are hoping for that is
apparently not in your immediate experience. Ponder
that hoped-for thing or experience, and breathe
into your body. As you are breathing into your
body, visualize your body, or if you are not adept
at visualization, feel your body. Ask to be shown
points of light in the body where there is blockage
that is associated with this hope that is not being
experienced in the prophetic present. Or ask for your
attention to be drawn to those points as a sensation
— pain, pressure, or hot or cold.

Wherever the brightest of the lights or the strongest
of the feelings is in your body, place your right hand
on it. If it is in your lower extremities, sit up to be able
to place your hand there. Then begin to tap that spot
firmly with your index, middle, and ring fingers. As
you are tapping, say to yourself: "In this place where
the body has generated a negative association to my
intended outcome, I release, on the first level, that
blockage. I release on the second level (deeper) the
blockage...." And then on down to the seventh level.
There, pause and simply breathe for a moment and
then ask again to be shown where blockages remain
in your body.

If the same spot still lights up or feels blocked, then
tap again and go eighth level, ninth level, tenth

level. Then, when you have completed, breathe into that spot once again. If that was the only blockage, you are done and you can then go to your regular meditation. If there is another area that lights up or another feeling perhaps not as strong, then you move to that next area. If you find that your body is so lit up with blockages that you cannot possibly get to all of it in one session, simply do the strongest of areas that is revealed.

One final step that is of greatest value is for you to affirm that you are working with the mortal form but that you are identified with your immortality, with the radiance that you are. Identifying with your Soul — as that infinite, immortal, intelligent radiance — you are simply directing your body to come into alignment with the Soul's values. In that way you close your session by bringing yourself back to your most expansive consciousness.

TEN LEVELS OF CONSCIOUSNESS

There are many systems of thought that try to describe the complex interactions between the body, the emotions, the mind, the light field and the universe, but none are quite as simple as this system.

The levels of consciousness are associated with the phases of evolution of the human species from single cell to the complex, highly evolved and interconnected body of all humanity. These ten levels are the underpinnings of the human experience. Blockages can happen on any one of these levels. Clearing a blockage requires conscious effort and attention.

1. Single cell — action/reaction

2. Reptile — fight or flight

3. Mammal — olfactory sense/intuition

4. Family — empathy

5. Tribe — judgment

6. Culture — shared values

7. Nation — higher order of values codified into law

8. Planet — emerging awareness of humanity as an organism

9. Solar System — awareness of planet as sentient being

10. Cosmos — emerging awareness of universal intelligence

An individual's consciousness rises as they move with their Soul's curriculum. For some, their greatest achievement of consciousness may be level seven, that of nation — coming to know right from wrong as it is codified within their culture or society. Some may rise further, growing into awareness, for example, that everything is Divine Intelligence (level nine — awareness of planet as sentient being). It is very rare that an individual remains at level one — this would be, basically, an individual who is a vegetable or only experiences a coma state, but is still a living organism.

As an individual moves through the levels in their maturation, trauma or stress can result in a blockage *at that level*. This is why it is valuable to have an awareness of the levels of consciousness. It can be helpful in identifying the blockage and clearing it.

You are living at a time on Earth when more individuals than ever are achieving the tenth level of consciousness — the emerging awareness of Infinite Intelligence. Understanding these levels of consciousness can provide you with a map as you meet the challenges of your Soul's curriculum.

The first time I used the blockage clearing exercise, I had trouble settling in and focusing. My mind kept wandering and I was unsure how to visualize something I was hoping for and stay focused on it. I realized that I wasn't trusting that the deeper intelligence within me would help guide me through the process. I was more concerned with "getting it right." When I let go of that, I noticed that there was a sensation of mild discomfort in my gut and in my throat. I decided that I would focus on those two areas and I started tapping.

I questioned whether I should start with the tenth level or the first level and whether I should think about the meaning of each level as I was tapping. Once again, when I let go and simply tapped and felt myself moving from a more current conscious state to deeper states of consciousness, I was able to relax and flow with the exercise. Less thinking proved to be better.

When I was done I felt more peaceful. I repeated the exercise whenever I felt as though I was reverting to longing or yearning instead of generating the state of consciousness of "having" in the prophetic present.

Instead of wanting and not having, the exercise provided me with a means to stay on track, building the desired consciousness within. I also then had the experience of that fulfillment appearing in the external.

It is the altered ego that struggles.

— *Solano*

Like an obedient pet, the altered ego begins to quiet
when the house has a firm master. There is no need for
struggle. Yet, reflect on how much is demanded of you
— getting an education, keeping house, raising children,
making a fortune, losing weight, being healthy and strong
— such things have required much of you and they,
ultimately, provide you with great satisfaction. It is like
going to see a film where the characters embark on an
adventurous journey, one that ultimately results in
wisdom. It is satisfying. It delights your Soul — understanding the path to wisdom and leading you there.

Should you strive for excellence in your career? You must
ask yourself, does it bring you joy? Is it satisfying? Do you
feel that you are learning about yourself and becoming
more Soulful, more identified with your immortality? If you
answered yes, then, indeed, it is an appropriate striving.
If you are frustrated and lost and feel as though you are
struggling and getting nowhere, it may be better to let it
go. The altered ego is what feels thwarted and frustrated.
It is the altered ego that experiences anger at the time
factor, for when one is a slave to time there is never
enough of it.

Look at your life, specifically your relationship to hope
and striving and the prophetic present. Are you capable
of bringing your hopes into the prophetic present —
generating feelings of fulfillment in the present? If you
are able to do that, you can neutralize the altered ego's
limitations. This will clear the way for you to more gracefully bring in what you wish to experience in the present.

Imagine that you truly know you are forever.

— *Solano*

THE ALTERED EGO'S PURPOSE

The altered ego does have a purpose. Though it may seem at times to have run amok, particularly when you are addled by fears and insecurities or when you look at your body for the millionth time and judge it. It can seem that the altered ego has gone astray when you compare yourself to others, when you yearn for love or touch or to simply have a moment of peace, or when the chattering mind constantly speaks of fears and angers, aging, the need for more money, more strength, more beauty, more time, more, more, more.

However, the way that the Soul and the altered ego work together is very elegant. The altered ego may try to achieve a Soulful state of consciousness, but instead constantly prompts emotions of insecurity because it knows that ultimately it will die with the body.

This is why it helps to identify your greatest insecurities. Identify where the repetitious thoughts are. Then, rather than recoil from those emotions, move into the pain. Deepen into that sense of insecurity or insufficiency. Settle in there, into that pain, that longing, that yearning, that

fear. Look at the images that are associated with those feelings. The faces. The surroundings. Listen to the voices and hear the familiar sounds. Now imagine a growing light, like a morning sun getting brighter and brighter in the sky. As the light increases all of the images begin to pale, to fade. The voices fade with them. It's as if the blazing white light is overpowering all of the other colors of the spectrum.

Your altered ego may insist that you must tend to your fears. But the Soul says, "Fear not, we are forever. Fear not, we are not bound by time and space. Fear not, for I will show you the way to a greater life, greater fulfillment, greater peace and joy."

If you isolate all of those places in your life where you remain identified with the altered ego and replace them with the conscious intent to lead a Soul-identified life, radiance then pours into your being and expresses itself outward. It is in this way that the altered ego and the Soul work together to move you into a more expansive state of consciousness.

The altered ego is a part of your creativity.

— *Solano*

It is important to keep in mind that the altered ego is not a liability. It is an asset. And much like an overprotective dog, it needs something to do to keep busy. Give your altered ego specific jobs in order to secure its cooperation. Those who have pets know that one of the best ways of living with a pet is for it to understand what its role is and what the parameters are. It needs consistency to understand those parameters.

Have the altered ego be responsible for tending those things that it is good at — tending the physical body and environment, taking care of finances, organizing things, communicating well with others. The altered ego knows about time and geography. It has at its beck and call the tools needed to interface with your culture because it understands protocol. Give it purpose. Not just to keep it mindlessly busy, but also to keep it creatively engaged. This, too, gives you a greater ability to embrace what is because you more profoundly understand that the altered ego will be looking after those details that are time-based and mortality-based.

DNA: Map to the Soul

Your Soul has drawn you to the circumstance
in which you manifest as a human.
— *Solano*

THE DESIRE FOR SINGULARITY

There is a value and, more importantly, a passion — a fervent question — that your Soul has about the experience of being singular. It is that fervent question and that passionate desire which draws you to the moment of conception.

You have likely had the experience of feeling a fervent passion for something and, seemingly miraculously, helpful individuals appear or circumstances present themselves, and you find yourself walking through a door that allows you to have the experience you desire.

So it is with the Soul — the architect of your body. Its tone and frequency of passionate desire prompts the dream of individuals — your parents — who allow you the opportunity of bringing a body into being. It is not as though you are peering down at the earth looking for an available womb and decide, "Ah, there, that will do!" It is more like a dream in which you passionately desire an experience and so the dream of your life on Earth is continually presented to you in accordance with your frequency. It is seemingly mysterious, but it is formulaic.

There are eighty thousand genes in your DNA and nearly three billion pairs of sequences. The intellect is not capable of tracking all of these simultaneously. Something other than your intellect must do the task and that is none other than the very essence that has acted as the architect of your manifestation into physical form, your Soul.

At conception, the four nucleic acids which make up a genetic code, ATCG ("A", Adenine pairs with "T", Thymine. "C", Cytosine pairs with "G", Guanine) begin to assemble the basis of your body's DNA. But, it is not as though you intellectually choose the sperm and the egg and begin to design, "I want A, C, T, and G here, and I want T, C, G, and A there," and so on until you have three billion pairs of DNA. Rather, you as a Soul passionately engaged in the desire for knowledge of yourself as a Divine consciousness, commence a journey. Your DNA is the direct reflection of the Soul's frequency and the "questions" it is holding. Because of this, your DNA is like a map to your Soul.

It is within your capacity to change your DNA.

— *Solano*

RAPPORT

In taking a human body, you use the material that is provided from sperm and egg and your Soul acts as an architect designing the sequences and will make certain choices specifically for rapport.

Rapport or empathy is hard-wired into the mammalian brain. The result of rapport, however, is the perpetuation of the herd consciousness. This can lead one to putter along in relative sameness lifetime after lifetime. To overcome the habitual drive for rapport, one must have a greater, more compelling desire, like the desire to awaken to your true nature. It requires examining the choices that you habitually make as a result of identification with the altered ego and choose instead the stillness afforded by identifying with your immortal self. You then begin to live in your body in such a way as to virtually change the sequencing of your DNA.

You achieve in this evolutionary leap an important development, not only for yourself, but also for your species. The more you become the Soulful self that you desire to be, the more you take that tone into your daily life, the more you inhabit Divine consciousness in every moment and the more humankind evolves as a species.

An imprint of perfect health exists in your DNA.

— *Solano*

THE IMPRINT OF PERFECT HEALTH

A human being has the ability to go through a devastating illness or injury, and yet access through their thoughts the genetic architecture of the body to make it whole again. There are documented examples of an individual's ability to overcome illness. You possess the ability to raise your body up into the frequency of light, disassemble it, and to reassemble it in another place. This, however, will likely require greater evolution of the species in order for it to be demonstrated with any regularity.

That which you can sustain in thought enough to generate the emotional experience of fulfillment you can achieve in the physical realm. Having generated the experience of fulfillment you create a magnetic field that resonates with that experience. The only thing that prevents you from being able, for instance, to sustain yourself at the peak of your physical expression throughout your life arc is the genetic predisposition to maintain rapport with your culture.

Followers of the Voodoo religion believe that the *evil eye* will imperil their lives. A death wish can cause them to sicken and die when cursed. But there are examples of something very similar in more advanced cultures. Statistics show that most people who are given a diagnosis of cancer view it as a death sentence. The same is true of heart disease. Each day as you read the newspaper, watch television, and chatter among yourselves, when you hear of someone who has succumbed to the prevailing consciousness of your culture, you are flirting with subscribing to that consciousness.

Instead of subscribing to a culture of illness and death, know that you are able to replicate precisely and unendingly the structure in your cells that holds you at your peak of strength, knowledge, and power. The way to do this is by passionately seeking the imprint of perfect health that exists in your DNA.

In many circumstances you are taught to simply accept ill health. You go to the doctor, she tells you that you are sick, and if you have questions, she refers to research, and that is all. Rarely are you told about individuals who, though on the brink of death, through determined thought have been able to be vital again. There are also examples where a person's nerves have been severed, supposedly rendering an individual incapable of walking — yet, they walk again. Others are able to enter a trance state before surgery. They experience no blood loss, no pain, and heal more rapidly than those who go about it the ordinary way. Every individual is capable of attaining such a state of consciousness.

It is through such focused, disciplined thought and meditation that you can inhabit the consciousness, the intelligence that is the architect of your body. Inhabiting that heightened consciousness provides you the ability to be in a constant state of rejuvenation. Therein arises the awareness that you have the ability to work with the architecture of your body and manifest it as you deem. Aligned with that consciousness you can manipulate your genetic material where your intellect cannot. The architect, the Infinite Intelligence within, is that part of you that possesses the capacity to disassemble your body and put it back together again.

Breaking rapport with the convention of aging
is achieved by letting your Soul-identified consciousness
reorder your DNA.

— *Solano*

AGING

Among the eighty thousand genes that manufacture the proteins which determine your hair color, body size, the tambour of your voice, much of your behavior, gestures, the way your body moves, what you crave, there is one which, due to your rapport with the prevailing culture, grows shorter and shorter with each replication of a cell. It is due to that shortening that you arise in the morning and look in your mirror and see another little wrinkle or the glint of white in your hair.

This is due to the consciousness within the cells in their process of dividing, agreeing with the convention of aging in your culture, and allowing that gene to be whittled away, bit-by-bit. The desire to sustain yourself in strength, in abundance of energy, in youthful appearance through all of your life is enough for you to be able to create a different consciousness. But it must be given unambiguous and focused support. When you arise and you see that little wrinkle, it is not for you to affirm the consciousness of aging, of rapport with your species. Instead, you must passionately seek to merge with the consciousness that unlocks the genetic material so that with each cell division that gene remains the same length.

It is not your intellect that allows you to go into each cell and single out that particular gene and have it remain the same length. It occurs through identifying with your Soul and fervently desiring the evolution so that the change is provided by the Soul, the architect of your DNA structure.

In prayer your fervent questions arise,

and the imagination is activated.

— *Solano*

INHABITING THE SACRED BORDERLAND

Everything that *is* is rendered into physicality through thought. The more you press into that knowledge, the more your meditations and your prayers provide access to the intelligence that is responsible for the creation of the body.

The moment you arise is the moment of greatest creative imprint in the flow of your day. It is a sacred time, for it is the borderland. It is the time when you can set the tone of the consciousness that you want to inhabit. Doing this requires fervent questioning — asking to know God in every moment, to hear God in every moment, to be one in every moment with the Divine. It is a moment for prayer. Invoke the knowledge that you are Divine, that in your divinity you have the capacity to manifest physically as you wish here on Earth.

If meditation is difficult for you, imagine an airtight sphere with no seams. No point of entry or exit. In that space let there be void, emptiness, filled with all possibility. Then in that space, imagine yourself seated in comfort, in perfect rest. Resting there allows you to be still. That is the point of meditation. Not to work over your latest project. Not to work over what your day is to be. Not to struggle to strategize what you will do to achieve your dreams, but rather to be still. It is in the empty space that your fervent desire can access the architect of your physical existence — the indwelling Infinite Intelligence.

If you cannot be empty and rest in the void, then listen to your breath and let that be a mantra, or use the mantra you've been given, or say simply, "God." "I am God." "I am God." Retreat to this place of stillness in the sacred borderland of the morning. Allow at least twenty minutes to go by. Then, before you begin your day, kneel down and place your forehead to the floor. Doing so, you signal your willingness to bow to the Infinite Intelligence. Then rise and begin your day and fervently hold this consciousness through each and every moment.

The moment before you sleep is another borderland. At that time, take a moment and once again bow to the Divinity that dwells within you. Bow down and touch your head to the floor. Acknowledge that you have lived another day, and have come closer to understanding what it is to dwell in Divine awareness every moment.

Keeping these rituals alive, what you achieve is the proper balance of fervent, prayerful desire to know, and the empty space in which knowingness can enter. You engage as well the ability to allow a new consciousness to settle into your being.

DNA MEDITATION

Make yourself comfortable. Loosen your clothing if necessary and still your body. Turn your attention first to your breathing. Notice the air coming in, and the transfer of oxygen in your lungs, giving your blood all that is necessary to fuel cellular reproduction. As you focus on your breath, allow yourself to become more and more at ease with your body. Release any residual stress and tension. Let your jaw be slack. Let your shoulders be heavy. Let your abdomen release all the way down to the pubic bone. Let the musculature in the abdomen be at ease.

You may want to record this meditation and play it back in a moment of relaxation.

As you are stilling yourself, create that perfectly seamless and utterly impenetrable sphere. And find yourself resting at peace in your body, gently, within this sphere. There, notice and appreciate the breath as it comes in. Notice how easily and gracefully it is exhaled from your body. And in this place of emptiness and stillness, call up one cell of your body, larger than life-size, to hover before you. Look upon it in wonder. Notice the spark of light that is in the nucleus of this cell. Notice the activity that continues, seemingly without your specific direction. Notice the way in which the chromosomes collect themselves, preparing to divide.

As the dance of the chromosomes is displayed, go deeper into this cell, diving into the strand of DNA that gives order to this cell and its reproduction. Notice the colors. Notice the geometric precision of the double helix. As you are watching, note that the processes of the cell continue. While viewing its exquisite beauty, allow yourself to merge with it. Let it become one with you, the observer, the consciousness. Now, in this state of oneness with this single cell, include all of the cells in your body. Feel the vibrancy of your body. Allow your body to shimmer with the activity that proceeds, seemingly without your direction. Now open the crown of your head and let the light of Divine Consciousness flood into your body. Let it fuel the process of cellular division. And as you experience the cellular replication being fueled by the light of the Divine, move deeper into your body, anchoring within. Once again notice your breath. Once again notice the sphere in which your body is safe and secure.

Now, place your thoughts once more on the cellular replication. Look at the way in which your cells have replicated themselves so precisely. See that this strand, this double helix, is utilizing the information that was programmed by your Soul in the precision of the original design. Into each moment draw in the light of the Divine. With each division, note that you are maintaining rapport with the Divine consciousness.

Then dive even deeper. You have pressed into the DNA within this one cell. And within the cellular structure of your entire body you have sought the light, the spark that sustains each cell. Now press deeper into that light such that it gives way to a great ocean, the Source of all. Discover here the essence that you are which transcends physical matter. Let that discovery generate a radiance within that begins to emanate out. Let this power move through the entirety of your body, the entirety of your consciousness, and through this door, allow yourself to experience oneness with all that is. Simply rest there. Notice the moments of emptiness. Allow yourself to begin to expand those moments of emptiness.

Gently return to your waking consciousness, allowing yourself to reincorporate. Notice that you bring with you a new stillness from having touched the emptiness within. Into that emptiness God, the Source, the Divine Mystery, may move and infuse your life with the energy that sustains your body. In that stillness, give thanks for this exploration.

Every moment you are imagining your life.

— *Solano*

DREAMING YOUR LIFE

Your imagination is one of the most important tools that
you have. As a child your entire life was imagination. You
were literally dreaming up your life. You looked at life and
everything was just so much color, light, shadow, sound,
and imagery — without names, without value. Entering
into that imagination again is an important part of your
process, for it is through your imagination that you can
generate the sort of emotional experience you desire for
this life.

I am not referring to
cars and relationships
and houses and things
of that sort. I refer to
your Soul's desire for
experience, knowl-
edge, and your grasp
of yourself as Divine.

If you were able to hold awareness of all that you know
about your culture, and your goals and ambitions, and at
the same moment be aware that you are dreaming your
body and imagining your life, you would be at a point of

empowerment. That empowerment would allow you to swiftly collect from this experience everything that you desire.

The more passionately you desire to experience yourself as divinity dwelling in flesh, the more your life will be an experience of being at the point of empowerment. That empowerment comes when you infuse into any given moment the knowledge that this is your dream. It comes in the moment when you realize that it is your consciousness that has created this picture, the body and the experience that surrounds you.

When you are rooted in your divinity, you have the opportunity to shift your reality, to enter a state of consciousness that will expand into your immediate environment and create a dream that is more precise to your Soul's journey. It affects your body first because that is the manifestation of your frequency. When you inhabit the consciousness you desire, the hormones re-sort themselves and the cells and the DNA respond differently. Then your magnetic field expresses itself differently; and the moment your magnetic field expresses itself differently, everything around you must shift. That is the way it works.

This moment, perfect health is possible.

— *Solano*

Polarities exist here on Earth — light and dark, vitality and decay, expansion and contraction. These polarities are part of your exploration here. You explore your shadow and your fears. You also explore your light, your exquisite awareness that you are forever. You have a challenge before you. Rather than trying to prevent yourself from aging and dying, the aim is to live fully awake in every moment. Recognize that when you dwell on your past or fear your future, you rob yourself of the ability to sit in your power source, the generator of your dream. That generator, the Soul, is accessible through the present moment alone.

At any moment, perfect health is possible in your body. It occurs by fully and completely recognizing that your body is born of Infinite Intelligence.

Time is a specific creation of this plane. The past — from which you derive your identity and which determines your body and its state of health — took place in a present moment. Present moment is all there is. The future only comes to be when it becomes present, and it is by inhabiting the present that you can access your Infinite Intelligence.

Why is it that ten people can be subjected to a virus, and only one or two contract that virus and become ill? Why is it that cancer cells exist in every single body on this planet, and only a small percentage of individuals actually develop cancer? It is the frequency of the individuals who are in the body, on their path of growth toward consciousness. Your Soul, following the curriculum it has designed, determines what you experience repetitively in terms of fear, toxicity born of negativity, and the way those thoughts interact with the body. It is that design that grants the wisdom that the Soul has come to seek from this lifetime in relation to the experience of being in a body.

The body is your teacher and this is a planet of demonstration. What that means, very simply, is that you come to this planet to demonstrate to yourself what wisdom you have gathered; whether you have mastered it, or whether you are still subject to negativity, fear, anger, violence, power, control, addiction, doubt, worry, insecurity. Those are negativities that build up in a body, but they are not what you are. You are the Soul — the consciousness engaged in the act of demonstrating to yourself your knowledge of this plane.

Recognize that your Soul has generated

a dream of a body for your growth.

— *Solano*

The key to physical mastery of this plane is to raise your vibratory frequency so that the DNA, the architecture of your body, can be sustained in good health and so that your path is marked by grace and peace.

To that end, never curse your body. Never hate it. Never be angry with it. Never judge it. Never look upon it with pity. Never fear it. Never do you want to look upon your body and assign to it failure. It matters not if you are suffering a disease. It matters not if you find yourself aging and frail. It is for you to look upon your body and to love it, to bless it, to recognize that it is conscious, to recognize that it is Divine Mind too. When you identify with your Soul and recognize that your Soul has dreamed the body, your relationship to your physical form becomes more graceful and your ability to affect change on the level of your DNA is enhanced.

Emotions

Your emotional state is not who you are.

— *Solano*

There are many ways in which individuals lose their connection to their Soul and their immortality and, thus, find
themselves resisting what is. Some veer off into imagined
or remembered conversations. Some get caught up in
music or images that run repeatedly in their thoughts.

Some simply get so caught up in the power of an emotion that they crave it more than anything else. Some find
themselves reacting to others' emotions. They are susceptible to others' feelings, the emotional tone of a roomful of
people, for example. They make that their life, rather than
anchoring themselves in that place of radiant immortality
that gave rise to their body to begin with.

Being sensitive to emotional frequencies is a skill that
can be harnessed, as is being adept at visualization. The
important thing to remember about such skills is that they
engage the process of creativity that manifests what you
experience as "reality." Be aware of what you are visual-
izing or hearing. You can then consciously direct each
visualization or fantasy so that you are choosing for it to be
in alignment with your prophetic present.

If, due to fears, you visualize or conjecture something that
you do not want, bring yourself to attention because that

is where the altered ego runs amok. In such moments, interrupt the process by saying to yourself, "I bless this vision (or imagined experience), and I release it *unmanifested*, back into the pure potential." This is a strategy for remaining seated in the now, while recognizing and valuing your creativity.

The same is true for those who sense another's emotions and embrace them as their own. Bring yourself to con-scious awareness. Send that emotion back into the pure potential, blessed, but not manifested, and seat yourself in your Soul, where all emotion is available to you as choice.

When all emotion is available to you as choice, what you will choose is bliss, joy, and peace, delight in your creativity, delight in your expression as One with all that is.

Identification with your Soul grants you the ability to
master your emotions rather than be subject to them.
— *Solano*

THE LIMBIC SYSTEM

Everything that you consider your "reality" is energy that manifests around you in response to your unique frequency. It is for that reason that emotions must be understood, as they are a key element in creating that frequency. Emotions are what most frequently anchor you to altered ego identification, especially the so-called negative emotions. In order to understand emotions, we must look at the physical body, especially your olfactory sense (smell), brain, central nervous system, and endocrine system, because they hold the keys to emotions as you experience them.

The Earth is an illusion that has been built by agreement. The collective consciousness, informed by science, by and large, agrees that life began with a one-celled organism. Those one-celled creatures then evolved to become more complex, until ultimately there were many life forms with great diversity expressing here on Earth. Fast-forward through the reptiles and all of that and we come to a point millions of years ago in the illusion of time in which the development of higher brain functions in mammals took place. That development was the precursor to some of the brain functions you now experience in your bodies.

One of the most important developments in mammals was that the olfactory sense began to be more important than sight as the means by which this illusion was perceived. The safety of the body was more effectively preserved through the use of the sense of smell. And it is the sense of smell in the mammalian brain that developed into what has become the limbic system in the brain. The limbic system is comprised of the hippocampus, amygdalae, anterior thalamic nuclei, septum, limbic cortex, and fornix. It is the seat of emotions as you now experience them. Your emotions, having grown out of the sense of smell, are body-based. Most particularly, so-called negative emotions are body-based.

Median section of the brain

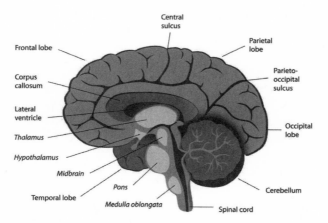

There are really only two main categories of emotion, pain or pleasure, prompted by a near instantaneous assessment of either impending annihilation or survival. Every emotion, no matter how complex, can be put into one of these two categories. The ancient humans, your genetic forebears, relied on the sense of smell most heavily to determine whether or not a situation, another animal or human, was likely to create pain or whether it was likely to create pleasure. Whether it was likely to result in annihilation or contribute to the survival of the body and thus, the species.

The altered ego is constantly evaluating. "What is this? I'm afraid of that. I love that. I want this." Much of its evaluation is based on your sense of smell. Even in those instances where you have an instinctual response to someone but have not had a conscious experience of smelling him or her, you received a subtle olfactory message about the person or the group or the place or the food with which you were engaging. In that moment as the limbic system in the brain begins to make its evaluation you have a very brief moment, the blink of an eye, in which to catch the thought, before the thought generates an emotion. That blink of an eye is the key to the hidden potential in your emotional processes.

If you have established an observer that watches your mental processes, you have the opportunity to determine if it is appropriate to respond to a stimulus emotionally. In your desire to come to consciousness this is probably the most important skill to gain.

It is in that blink of an eye that you have the opportunity to drop into the space prior to your altered ego's reactions. There, instead of assigning frustration or fear or irritation to the stimulus, you remind yourself that you are more than your body and your thoughts and emotions. You are that which survives the body. You are that which survives annihilation. You are forever. You are your Soul.

THE BLINK OF AN EYE

When you explore emotions such as anger, spite, envy, jealousy, insecurity, fear — emotions that move you out of your center and into an identity based on fear and mortality, you move deeper into singularity. Emotions that prompt you to feel alone and singular are inevitably a wild ride. There, you are at effect of all stimuli rather than being able to receive stimuli and remain centered in your being. When you remain centered you have the ability to be wise and grounded, capable of making decisions that lift the frequency of the emotion and provide you with the ability to feel unconditional love, peace, and joy. Dwelling there allows you to elevate the frequency of your light field. The higher your frequency the more your life becomes one of ease and grace, abundance and simplicity.

Each day, with few exceptions, you arise in an emotional state. Either you feel a sense of well-being, or you feel anxious. You feel peaceful, or lusty, or frightened. It is preferable in that moment to evaluate what you are feeling and to observe it. In that way you drop into that "blink of an eye" moment and reestablish yourself as one with your Soul, and not at effect of your emotional life.

The wild ride of emotion is precisely what some individuals most want. It is what makes a life colorful for them and precisely what — and this is a key point — grants them a sense of identity.

For them the part that is constantly evaluating stimuli in an effort to keep them safe from annihilation dominates their life moment to moment and prompts them to identify more with singularity. The more this happens, the more they are subject to the temporal nature of life, because their life becomes all about their personality, body, age, relationships, job, their level of accomplishment.

Conversely, if you are one who embraces the knowledge that change is all there is and that you are immortal, constantly evolving, constantly growing, constantly changing, but eternal, you identify with the Oneness of all life and you begin to be in a position of choice about emotions. Your emotions then reveal another hidden potential, the potential to teach you the difference between altered ego identity and Soul identity.

Being identified with your expansive,
Divine self, yet still dwelling in a human body,
is the most potent way of living.

— *Solano*

EMPATHY

There are times when an emotion will pass through you that you cannot identify as having come from the evaluation of obvious stimuli. This may be due to emotional states that begin with another individual or group. Let's say that an individual who is in a position of great power generates an emotion. That emotion may then cascade through the consciousness of the entire global neural network — the empathic interconnectivity of humans the world over. The shift in the electromagnetic field of the greater human tribe can affect the endocrine system of you, the individual.

Your brain has evolved to be empathic. Empathy can be defined as "enlightened self-interest." In the evolution of humanity, the ability to take care of offspring and the tribe allowed the human species to not just survive, but thrive. It is a fundamental aspect of your life in a body that must not be overlooked in examining the hidden potential within emotion.

Becoming aware of the phenomenon of empathy, whether you live in a city or in isolation, allows you to begin to notice when you experience fear that is generated because of a crisis that is perhaps half way around the world.

It is important to keep this in mind when you awaken. Before you begin to assess your emotional state with your linear mind, drop into the space between your thoughts and establish your identity as the Soul that you are, potent in your creativity to build the life that you wish to dream. It is in this space that you can begin to be aware of what emotions you are generating and what emotions are generated by the consciousness of humanity in which you are dwelling.

That moment when you first awaken, remind yourself that everything around you — walls, other bodies, trees, and plants, the Earth beneath you — is all energy creating an illusion. Therefore it is pliable. But in order to change it you must first establish the frequency that you wish to dwell in — the frequency of immortality. Become present in your body and aware that your Soul transcends time and space. You, then, are able to choose what you desire to create, and what emotions you desire to experience.

Drop into the space between thoughts and establish

your safety based on your immortality.

— *Solano*

THE OLFACTORY SYSTEM

The endocrine system is linked inextricably with scent in a human body. You perceive scent and that then prompts reaction. You are constantly receiving information from your olfactory sense. You smell one another and your environment, whether you are aware of it or not. From that sense of smell you make assessments about your safety and well-being.

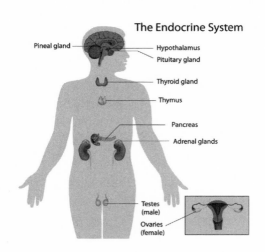

The Endocrine System

To heighten your ability to perceive at this level requires discipline and attentiveness. For example, if you enter a room that is familiar to you, do not ignore your olfactory sense because you feel safe in that room. Take a moment and place your attention on your nose. Focus on the nerves as they extend from your olfactory bulbs up into the hypothalamus. The hypothalamus is an extremely important part of the limbic brain. The limbic brain in relationship to the hypothalamus is responsible for the hormone flow in the body.

When you catch a scent, whether the scent is due to the change in frequency of the human herd at large or the approach of an individual whom you instantly mistrust, the hypothalamus is responsible for the adrenals in your body secreting hormones and prompting in the body the fight or flight syndrome.

This process is constantly at work, generating your emotional life. The key is to remember that you always have choice whether or not to feel the emotions that are generated by the olfactory sense stimulating the hypothalamus, and in turn stimulating the hormones in the body. The moment that you smell something that may result in an emotional reaction, it is wise to drop into the space between thoughts and feel your sense of safety based on identification with the Soul.

It is a more effective way of living. Dropping into the space between thoughts and remembering yourself to be forever, you have the opportunity to make choices and decisions, but more importantly to be the frequency that you want to consistently maintain. It is through this determined action that you maintain a conscious relationship with your Soul that perceives everything that is generated in your experience as being plentiful.

Agnieszka Sorokowska, a doctoral candidate at the University of Wroclaw in Poland, along with her colleagues, asked thirty men and thirty women to don white cotton t-shirts for three consecutive nights. Participants could not use fragrances, deodorants, or soaps, and could not smoke or drink or eat odorous foods during the study. Participants also took a personality test.

Shirts from the "odor donors" were collected and rated by 100 men and 100 women. Raters were asked to smell the shirts (placed in non-transparent plastic bags) and evaluate five personality traits of the donors, on a scale of one to ten. Each rater assessed six shirts, and twenty raters assessed each shirt.

The judges' ratings matched up with the self-assessments of the donors for three personality traits: extroversion (the tendency to be outgoing and sociable), neuroticism (the tendency to feel anxious and moody), and dominance (the urge to be a leader).

The matches were far from perfect. But the raters predicted the donor's level of extroversion and neuroticism through smell about as accurately as participants in a different study predicted personality traits based on a video depicting a person's behavior, Sorokowska said.

Judgments of dominance were most accurate in the case where an individual rater was assessing the odor of someone who was the opposite sex, suggesting such judgments are especially important when it comes to choosing a mate, the researchers said.

Extroversion, neuroticism, and dominance are all traits that may, to some extent, be expressed physiologically, including through our emotions.

For instance, people who are neurotic may sweat more when they experience stress, which would modify the bacteria in their underarms and make them smell different, the researchers said.

Personality traits may also be linked with the secretion of hormones that could alter a person's scent. People who are high in dominance may have higher levels of testosterone, which in turn may modify their sweat glands, the researchers said.

You create the electromagnetic field
around you that creates your reality.
— *Solano*

THE CELLULAR EFFECT OF EMOTIONS

When disturbed and erratic due to emotional states, the electromagnetic frequency of your light field creates more disturbances in your life — mishaps and collisions — literal and figurative. Electromagnetic disturbances in your light field can affect electronics, computers, machinery of all kinds, and most importantly your interactions with other people and animals. This will cause events that upset the flow of grace in your life. It is for you to determine whether to master your emotions and settle the disturbance, or whether you simply wish to play in that realm of reaction and drama.

The complexity of your emotions is due to all of the stimuli you receive, whether it is tactile or visual, olfactory, gustatory, or auditory input. The body receives all of this stimuli and the limbic brain then begins to assess and respond. The central nervous system then fires off cellular messages in response to the stimuli. Eventually a body grows weary of the accumulation of firings within the cells. This is one of the reasons that deep rapid eye movement (REM) sleep is necessary, to reset the body on a cellular level.

Humans on the whole are drawn to experiences that are emotionally charged — horror movies or romance novels, for example. As fear is a predominant emotion on Earth, it is sought out frequently to try to gain a handle on it. If that is done at an early age, an identity based on fear is etched deeply into the central nervous system and it becomes an addiction.

When that happens, an individual expects to be afraid and actually craves the hormones created by fear. Then the cells get fatigued from the constant state of alarm and the individual wants to shut down. That is often when an individual turns to stimulants or depressants to provide a change of state.

But neither stimulants nor depressants effectively clear the cell of the accumulated charge. They simply dull it, leaving the accumulated charge to have to be dealt with at another moment. So if you find yourself drawn to an addiction, whether it is food, tobacco, alcohol, or sex, remember that those things which you addict to that change the chemistry of your body are attempts to clear the cells on that level.

Yoga, Tai Chi, aerobic exercise, dancing — all are effective ways to clear the cells of accumulated toxicity. If you don't have the ability for such exertion, then engaging in a meditative breathing practice is another way to accomplish the clearing.

Meditative breathing practice addresses the clearing of the cells of the charge of fear. Whether it is exercise, or a breathing practice, if it is engaged as a means of becoming Soul-identified it will help to keep the body up to date, refreshing it on a cellular level so that you are able to dwell in the present moment, Soul-identified.

*Learning a formal meditation technique was very important
for me when I was living in New York City. I felt I needed
something to calm myself in my over-stimulated life.
Transcendental Meditation seemed like a perfect match
for me. I was very suspicious of gurus or certain religious
groups that required devotional rituals. And I didn't
believe the money they asked for regularly could secure
for me the secrets of enlightenment. With TM, I was able
to learn the technique and then practice it on my own.
That suited me just fine.*

*Once I'd been initiated and knew the pathway, it was a
matter of setting aside the time twenty minutes two times
daily to sit and meditate. I found no difficulty in doing this,
as the respite from my overactive mental chatter and the
opportunity to relax out of my normal state of high alert
was welcome.*

*The thing that was most notable at first was that while
meditating, spontaneous memories would surface, often
with resultant twitches or involuntary spasms in my
body, particularly in my abdomen. This went on for many
months, but eventually tapered off. Even now, after thirty-*

five years, I still sometimes experience this, but it is no longer mysterious to me. I know that what is happening is that nerve impulses have built up a charge in the cells of my body and when given the opportunity they "fire" and release, clearing my central nervous system and giving the cells the opportunity to recharge and rejuvenate.

Emotions provide the measure of your identification
with your Soul.

— *Solano*

THE HIDDEN POTENTIAL

Your emotions constantly provide you feedback about whether you are living your life centered in your Soul or whether you constantly perceive your life through the altered ego's limited perspective. This is the hidden potential in your emotions. If the bulk of your emotions tend to be fearful and angry, those emotions are providing you feedback that you are identified with the body, not your Soul, and that your emotions are being affected by the accumulated emotional charge in your cells.

Such feedback would indicate that you need a practice, at the least a meditative practice, to begin to release the accumulated emotional charge in the cells and to discover that "blink of an eye" where you can move into the observer position instead of careening off into an emotional response that floods the body with hormones and results in an erratic light field.

Keeping a journal of your emotional life is a way of understanding what the prevailing emotions are that you experience each day. Simply stop once an hour and ask yourself what you are feeling. It doesn't take long, but it provides you with an excellent reflection of the perspective in which you dwell in your life.

The Art of Loving Relationships

Seeking to know yourself through the reflection of others,

you realize who you are in your Divine essence.

— *Solano*

From the very earliest of moments you have been exploring emotions and what it is to be in relationship to
others. You explore your relationship to the Source by the
exploration of relationship to others — the exploration of
love. Few explorations reveal your emotional life to you as
pointedly as does relationship. By exploring relationships
with others, you ultimately come to understand that what
you seek is love of self.

When you were a child, you learned that you were
described by boundaries. As you began to see yourself as
an individual, you identified others as individual as well.
You then began to understand that it is important to have
love, or what you understood as love, to keep you safe.
Then a desire to possess and to control love was born.

Coming to understand yourself as an individual, desiring
to have love, desiring to be safe, desiring to be able to
express love, triggers the desire for possession which can
initiate issues of control, jealousy, anger, hatred — emotions born of the altered ego's view of mortality. In that
process you begin to engage love that is conditional. It is

conditioned on responses, on getting what you want — a sense of security, the ability to receive sustenance, food, warmth, touch — because these elements are part of the illusion of growth in the human body.

Moving from conditional love to unconditional love allows
you to be unshakable in the face of turbulent change.

— *Solano*

BEINGNESS

You live in a highly wired and interconnected world. Humanity is in the midst of massive change, turbulence, and revolution in government, weather, conflict between nations, and finance. The urgency in moving from conditional love to unconditional love is that by lifting your vibratory frequency you can fully inhabit self-love, love as reflected to you from the Divine Source. Doing so allows you to be unshakable in the face of turbulent change.

Think of a forest. Now think about one great tree in that forest. That extraordinary monolith grew from a seed. It did so by being itself, by following its own programming for creativity; in other words, by following its Soul's curriculum, its mandate for growth.

That monolith does not dwell there alone. It dwells within the context of a system, one in which there are creatures, other trees, plants, vines.

There is also the matrix in which it grows: the Earth, the water, the air, the light. All of these things are a part of its system, yet it is unique, like no other. It is not judgmental of itself, but rather simply *is* itself.

The tree dwells in a *beingness*. It is not rocked in its opinion of itself by the bird that nests in its branches. It is not altered in its mandate for growth by the insects that inhabit its bark, the microbes that are a part of it, or the lichens or the moss, the storm that comes and blows it this way and that. Even if a branch breaks off it is not altered in its beingness. If another tree struggles to grow greater than it, it simply follows its mandate: to reach for the light, to utilize the resources of the Earth to grow itself. If another tree falls on it and scars its bark, the bark repairs itself. If a vine fills its branches and tries to drag it down, it reaches for the light, draws up the water from the Earth, and follows its mandate. If there is a moment where there is not enough rain, it follows its mandate. It is itself, it dwells in its beingness.

This is an important metaphor because the key to the art of loving relationships is to follow your Soul's mandate to understand yourself as Divine. The Divine spark within you comes to this planet to manifest as a human among other humans. Think of them as a forest. You must follow your mandate to grow great, tall, strong, and to repair when it becomes necessary, but above all to follow your mandate. Your mandate is to know yourself as Divine.

Unlike trees or rocks or birds or insects, you have the potential to judge yourselves. Rather than simply understanding your mandate and following it, you often take circuitous routes in trying to understand the beingness of love.

Love is kindred to the Divine.

— *Solano*

MAGNETIC COHESION

Love is a magnetic cohesion that allows for creativity. In the context of a relationship to a parent, a sibling, a friend, or lover, love is often used as a means of getting something from someone else. In order to achieve this, you are usually required to give some semblance of that same thing in exchange. It is a highly conditional equation. And the equation is set up in so many different ways, in unspoken contracts that individuals create within their family, in relationships that are based on lust or hope of procreation, or relationships based on financial participation and obligation.

This is not Love. This is commerce, built on agreements based on conditions. In such relationships, the altered ego follows a circuitous route guided by its understanding of love. The altered ego is responsible for categorizing love as romantic love, or family obligation, or a compatible relationship in which one is part of a tribe or a community. Conditions are set up. The altered ego, understanding that there is something it wants, begins to observe the behaviors of others and notices that by manipulating your behavior or the behavior of others, "love" is given. If the others do not give the required behavior, then "love" is withheld. And if criticism or coldness is the response, how can love be returned?

Most have experienced what it is to "fall in love." Some have even made the commitment to another for a lifetime. Many have had the experience of finding an individual who feels so familiar that they are called the "Soul Mate." And many have, in these experiences, been severely disappointed.

Rather than a lifetime of joy, conversation, understanding and commitment, what they find instead is betrayal or irritation, vexation, control, and in some instances, abuse. But the Soul's mandate never flags. It will go on whatever circuitous journey your altered ego takes, and will work with it to move you along to understand the curriculum ordained when you came into this lifetime. All the while, love provides the magnetic cohesion that offers up this experience to you.

Alex had experienced a lifelong fear of being alone. In one of our sessions he told me that as a young man he suffered from severe loneliness. That was his pain. That was the thing that dominated his emotional landscape.

As he matured, he was successful at making friends, he did well in college, but what he longed for more than anything was for someone to come along who would fill that aching hole of loneliness. He longed for a partner.

What then ensued as he moved out on his own was a string of attempts at building a lasting and durable relationship. The first significant relationship ended in betrayal after a little more than a year. The second relationship ended after three years. This time Alex was the betrayer. The third significant relationship was highly dysfunctional despite being based on a shared belief that the two had similar spiritual values. That relationship ended after the two had tormented one another for five years, much of that time struggling to get out of the relationship, but highly addicted to one another.

He found himself alone again at thirty-five. Though he found himself dealing with the fear of being alone that he had always known, there was something else too. He was exhausted by what his fear of being alone had caused him to put up with in his life. The exhaustion resulted in Alex turning his attentions elsewhere.

He was offered a promising job and he found a small studio apartment and set about the task of making it comfortable. Every morning he would wake up and get in the car to drive to work. He told me that most every morning on the way to work he would cry. He would choose music that prompted sadness because he had heard that there was a value in contacting one's grief on a regular basis rather than trying to avoid it or cover it up. So this daily ritual was intentional, conscious, not out of his control.

What became clear in our work together is that at that time he was consciously surrendering and deepening into his fear of being alone.

Then one morning on his way to work, listening to one of his favorite albums, the saddest of his sad songs, there were no tears. He noticed that instead of loneliness or fear, he felt something quiet. When he got home that evening, he went for a walk in a nearby park and something happened that astonished him. He found himself not just at peace with being alone, but he felt an overwhelming sense of joy and fullness bubbling up from deep within and filling his entire body.

This sense of fullness stayed with him for many days, and the change in his outlook on life was apparent to all who knew him.

What happened next was particularly surprising. Within two weeks time of him having surrendered to "what is" he met, seemingly by chance, a man and they fell in love. Last I heard, they had been together for twenty years and still had a vibrant, creative, and fulfilling relationship.

Relationships are a master class
in coming to know oneself as Divine.

— *Solano*

DIVINE CREATIVITY

When you feel the desire for embrace, the desire to know
an individual more deeply, the desire for union, the desire
to build a life together, have a home, perhaps have a family,
you are being presented with an opportunity. The reflection
presented in your lover's face is your face, the face of God.
When you understand this, you taste the flavor of Divine
love. Only then can you set off on a journey of Love in a
balanced way.

When you realize that your divinity is being reflected in
your beloved's eyes, you recognize that it is not their role
to love you. It is not their role to keep you safe. It is not
their role to sacrifice to you. It is not their role to inhibit
their own growth to keep you happy. If we remove all
of the altered ego's concepts of love, if we remove the
altered ego's definitions of passion, what you are left
with is the Soul's determination that you will enter into
a journey with another being to grow. Period. Nothing
more, nothing less. To offer some alternative definition of
love, to lace it with golden threads and flowery phrases
would be a disservice.

Love *is* Divine creativity. It is sourced from within you. It is best expressed unconditionally because in expressing love unconditionally, you reflect to yourself unconditional love of yourself. That is very much like that monolithic tree. It is as though the tree loves itself unconditionally, and in loving itself unconditionally every moment it is in its Divine creativity. It is possible for you to dwell there as well.

MEDITATION ON UNCONDITIONAL LOVE

Drop down into your core, down into your Soul.
There, seated in your Soul, feel yourself as a point
of consciousness dwelling in a body, and that body
dwelling in the context of this particular dream,
this illusion. Everything and everyone around you
is a reflection of you — you dreaming you — in this
context. You, in your Soul, are not separate from the
Divine. You are the Divine One.

Hold onto that center, that stillness. Now think of an
individual with whom you are in a loving relationship,
or with whom you have been in a loving relationship.
It does not matter if that relationship is smooth or is
rocky, simply contemplate that relationship. Anchored
still in your Soul, seeing the face of that individual,
simply imagine dwelling in beingness in relation
to that other individual. Imagine yourself capable
this moment of loving that other unconditionally,
expecting nothing of them, not expecting particular
behaviors. Expecting nothing of yourself, nothing
but simply dwelling in Divine creativity. This may
cause fear if you are engaged in the altered ego's
understanding of contractual obligations and sacrifice
within relationship, expecting it of the other and
expecting it of yourself .

If you experience fear, then imagine that the other is
simply another monolithic tree in a forest in which

you both dwell and in which you are deeply and profoundly engaged in your beingness. Not judging yourself, not judging the other. Simply dwelling in Divine creativity. Take a moment with this imagery, and with the feelings that have been prompted, and set a marker here that this is the ideal; that this is a state of consciousness to refer to when you find yourself in relationship difficulties. There is much to discover here if you return to this consciousness again and again in your meditations.

The Soul understands that a relationship is a journey with another being for your growth.

— *Solano*

ENERGY STRUCTURES

An aspect of the altered ego and its control of the body rarely examined is the energetic structures created between you and another individual. Patterns of energy develop in the non-physical realm, creating energy structures — sometimes a wall, sometimes a maze. Various geometrical structures are designed in energy fields, between you and another person or persons. These energy fields are detectable with certain devices, such as the superconducting quantum interference device. But that is not what's important here. You can perceive such structures yourself and determine whether they serve you or not.

Think about an individual in your life with whom you have or have had contention. Think about those moments when you find yourself in a repetitious argument or judgment. Reflect on the physical space between you and that person. Experience that physical space nonlinearly, so you are not just talking to yourself about it, but you are feeling it. Scan it with your intuition. Notice the energy. And notice that it isn't just one-sided. What is built between you is the result of a collaboration. Claim your part of the responsibility for that structure, that energy field. Claiming it is an important key to being able to transform those emotional situations that plague you for days or months or years on end.

The simplest way to dismantle an energy structure that has been built between you and another individual is to open your heart, and with your heart open imagine, feel, or visualize building a bridge of light between your heart and theirs. Likely, you will feel the gravity of the old energy structure. But if you insist on keeping your heart open and connecting directly with their heart, eventually the old structure will break down; the relationship will change.

The means to intervene in your altered ego's process of creating unhealthy emotions or prompting the secretion of the hormones in your body that articulate themselves as your emotions, also applies to this circumstance. You have to catch your altered ego in the act of generating the thoughts. You have to understand that you are the one empowering it. You, in your altered ego, give life to your emotional reactions, and thus create the energetic structures that define your relationships.

Examine a relationship in your life that you wish to improve. The elements are you, the other person, and the dynamic. Not simply the emotions that flow back and forth, but the structure, the rigidity, the thought form that actually gets built energetically between you and the other person. The dismantling of that form requires that you understand that your altered ego is responsible for having built that structure.

For many, their altered ego would have them believe that the other person is responsible for the way that they feel. If the altered ego is brought to an understanding about the dynamic which closed the heart, activated the adrenal glands, restricted the throat and then shut off the capacity for the pituitary or pineal gland to function at all, then it can be taught to reverse the process.

One of the most important things is to understand that you do not live in a vacuum. Your emotional states have an impact on your light field, which then impacts all that surrounds you. Indeed, they define your created reality. More awareness of your emotional states can result in clear lines of engagement with other sentient beings that then results in a light field that resonates with greater joy and peace.

The quest for love is often an issue presented to Solano for guidance. People want to know when they will meet their perfect mate. Here, Solano offers his perspective on love to an individual seeking counsel:

"The emotions you feel stem from a habituation to the drama of striving to be loved, striving to be affirmed in that way. And that habituation, whether you are able to perceive it in this moment, is actually something that you have built your identity upon and therefore are attached to.

It is far more important for your growth to confront and embrace this knowledge than it is to eek out a tidbit of comfort or solace from a relationship. This dynamic in your life is the one that keeps you asleep, keeps you from feeling your glorious beauty and grace, it is the one which, by choosing it again and again, affirms that, rather than life being a sumptuous banquet of delight and love and connection and fulfillment, it is a constant struggle for affirmation that you are worthy of love.

Keep in mind, the emotions you feel this moment — yearning, hunger, longing, desire, lust, sadness — they are all generated within you, by you. If this moment you knew, really knew, that love, connection, sensual and erotic fulfillment were yours in abundance, it would not matter whether this person was available and desirous of seeing you or not. You would be anchored in the present moment and available to all the gifts that life has to offer and not focused on one avenue of fulfillment in the form of this one Soul. That, you see, is very much the result of programming. You have been taught that you are supposed to "catch" a mate. You must do everything within your power to look right, act right, smell right, walk right, have just the right amount of fiery lust and the right amount of virtue. This is all fantasy. It is the stuff of fairy tales.

Here is what is so, especially now as you are growing into the awareness of yourself as a spiritual being: relationship — whether it is long-term or a brief sexual encounter — is a tool of growth for your reflection.

Every being is an intelligent consciousness, whatever degree of awareness they possess of that. As such, they are like a magnet moving through life either repelled by other magnets or drawn to other magnets... because of the frequency of their light field. The tone, the frequency of your light field determines what you draw to you. You can raise the frequency of your light field and you can lower the frequency. Self-love, self-respect, self-fulfillment, self-awareness, love of life, love of the Divine Consciousness, awareness that what you have created is correct for your life because you grow from it — these things raise the vibratory frequency of your light field. These things make its magnetic quality more coherent to draw to you friends, colleagues, mentors, teachers, and, yes, lovers who are a match for that frequency.

Fear, self-doubt, affirmation of unattractiveness, self-judgment, worry, fear of rejection, neediness, superficiality, emptiness, sexual addiction — these traits lower one's vibratory frequency, and the corresponding situations and people will be of a lower frequency as well. And usually, there is corresponding drama due to the frequency in which the participants interact.

You are at a point where you are reaching for very different values — Soulfulness, connection, generosity, kindness, compassion, intuition, and creativity. In this period of transition, some of the old programs are stubbornly trying to have their way. This situation is an example — the altered ego has believed that the solution to all anxiety and insecurity is a relationship and it is trying desperately to make it happen. It is all the more desperate because it believes there is an expiration date on the possibility for that happiness. It believes that you are in a downward spiral of desirability and that this has to happen now, or else it won't happen at all. The altered ego actually would like to be swept up in a force greater than it (a relationship) so that all of the decision-making is taken out of its hands. But that is not appropriate to your life.

What is appropriate is for you to stop the leakage from your heart and your solar plexus, your adrenal glands and your loins. You are leaking energy from these chakras due to the habitual desire for another to come along and be the fulfillment that you seek, to comfort you, to take away the stress, the longing, and the insecurity. But none can do that. You may love another, feel lust, but in order for the leakage to stop and the magnetism of your light field to grow, you must face your own habitual need and realize that no one — NO ONE — can ever fulfill that need. Only you, in relationship to the Divine, can fill you up. Others then, when you are full, are simply mirrors to you of your fullness, your wholeness.

You are your salvation. You are the healer of your emotions. You are your hope and fulfillment.

Raise yourself up so that your magnetic field becomes more rhythmic and compelling... clear. But above all, be full of your sweetness, your tenderness, your innate beauty, your creativity, your intelligence. Fill yourself up with your uniqueness and let that draw to you what will come. Your altered ego does not know, nor will it ever know, the means to achieving fulfillment — or love for that matter — because it is too busy fearing its inevitable demise, and therefore will always see life through that lens.

Your task is to identify with your Soul that only knows forever and only knows plenty. Sitting there, in that identity, this moment of exquisite pain and longing, is simply part of the delicious experience of life in human body."

When you dwell wholly in Self Love,
your resonance draws to you loving interactions,
beauty, and outrageous creativity.

— *Solano*

LOVING SELF

For some individuals the master class in the art of loving relationships may be about being alone and content, dwelling simply in a place where they are, in their being-ness, joyful, fully engaged, delighted with themselves. But, if you are alone, you must ask yourself whether you are dwelling in a fortified world where others cannot enter.

It is a time in humanity's progress in which unconditional love is needed as the antidote to the forces that are inclined toward greater rigidity and hatred and control. The more you see division in your society, the more that you must redouble your efforts to inhabit unconditional love. This means loving those who are not able to love themselves enough to feel safe confronted with other ideas, other behaviors, other beliefs.

The art of loving relationships begins within you. Your job is to love yourself, and whenever you lose your way, bring yourself back to that. You must put your attention on loving you. That will allow all of the other frequencies around you to become orderly, in alignment with the frequency that you are anchoring, which is unconditional love.

When you dwell there wholly in love of Self, that magnetic resonance will draw to you, repeatedly, loving interactions, loving consciousness, beauty, light, and outrageous creativity. The Soul constantly dwells in such a state natively. Coming into alignment with the Soul's understanding of Love makes it abundantly clear that you always dwell in the Fields of Plenty.

Gaining Ground

Every seeming loss is experienced by the Soul

as the gaining of wisdom.

— *Solano*

Even when you experience what the altered ego feels
is loss — loss of health through aging or illness, loss of
money, a home, a pet, friends, relationships, loved ones
— each loss is a counterpoint to what is always occurring
within your Soul, which is the gaining of wisdom, and the
opportunity for greater peace. Ultimately, through such
loss, you gain an understanding that you are not separate,
not alone, not in peril, not in a blind alley, not dwelling in
lack, but rather, moving along very appropriately to your
Soul's aim for any given lifetime or experience.

The aim is to discover how you can know, on more than
just an intellectual level, that you are dwelling in plenty no
matter what the appearances are — to understand it deep
in your bones. It is possible to so deeply embrace it that
the knowing infuses itself into every fiber of your being,
and so that you carry that knowledge into every interaction, every experience that you have in your life.

So many people were caught in the financial upheaval of the global economic downturn. Where once they had experienced plenty, satisfied that their lives were being lived in harmony with spiritual and physical abundance, they found themselves catapulted into crisis and despair. Homes were foreclosed. Careers ended. And many of my dearest friends had to start over, late in life, trying to find a way back to financial security.

Clearly they were being tested in their spiritual beliefs and in their basic understanding of metaphysics. At the behest of several clients, I scheduled a seminar to address the issue. It was called "The Test."

As I sat in the ferry line, waiting to return to my island home, I pondered the upcoming workshop and what peace Solano's counsel could offer when so many had been stripped of everything they had.

Arriving home was always a joy, as my home sat in absolute solitude, protected by a forest of evergreen trees. Up a long, winding driveway you could see the house as you approached. Its distance from the hustle bustle always brought me feelings of safety and peace.

But this day ended any illusion of safety. While I was gone, someone had broken in through the downstairs media room. Splintered off its hinges was a door that was never locked. The office and lower rooms were ransacked. The culprits had hauled away everything of value. Gone were all the computers, monitors, the video cameras and gear, the photographic equipment, the television, and a long list of other things. Shock turned to anger, then to despair, then to grief. There was no "blink of an eye" moment here. Everything I needed to do my work as a filmmaker was stolen. My computers held book proposals, scripts, archives of past writings, things I treasured as a writer.

Police were called and insurance claims were made, everything one does to meet the needs of such a crisis. But what I could not address, or come to any real sense about was… why did this happen? Where once I felt protected and safe, I now felt vulnerable and at the effect of others. Using the lessons I knew from years of working with Solano, I had to remember… there are no mistakes. But what value could this possibly have? Then it dawned on me — I had been thrown into my own "test."

I began by accepting that I was being called out by my Soul to pay attention and to awaken on some level where I needed greater awareness. With that acceptance I managed to gain a little bit of neutrality, enough to begin to recognize that I was safe, things are just things and can be replaced. But still, I wanted to know the cause of this very anomalous event in my life.

I've found that the process of understanding my Soul's curriculum requires being willing to look unflinchingly at every aspect of my dream. It also helps to adopt the observer's attitude, as if my own life is a movie that I am analyzing.

I thought about what was stolen. Mostly it was the equipment that I relied upon for the production company, with the notable addition of the laptop that contained untold irretrievable amounts of archived writings. In other words, my identity as a writer and filmmaker had been stolen. What was the message there? I considered the possibility that this event was designed to strip away external claims of identity. In other's lives, I've observed that it is then that the deeper self, the essential self, is more clearly revealed.

I revisited my reasons for doing what I do — writing and making films. In the process I committed myself to maintain that work. I love writing and creating film projects to affect the greater consciousness. No matter what was stolen, I felt that this was my work to continue. And relatively quickly on that count, I came to balance. Whatever was lost could be replaced, or some earlier draft of a book found or rewritten and, likely, improved in the process.

After a few days it felt like I'd regained some degree of balance. Then I received a phone call from the deputy who had initially filed the report. The police had raided a "meth house" on the island. During the raid they found and confiscated a large number of computers and electronics. He felt it was most likely that the items were mine. Instead of following normal procedures and storing the items as evidence, he asked me to come and retrieve my belongings.

Almost everything was returned — a rare event after a burglary of this kind, I later learned.

Regardless of having my belongings returned, the process of understanding what happened continues to this day. What I've come to understand, at least partly, is that sometimes things are taken from us because their frequency needs to change. Or, said another way, an individual's frequency is constantly changing and the "stuff" around them, which manifested at a previous moment, holds a frequency that may not be appropriate to the current moment.

Life is a constant process of letting go, even when you think you are in the process of building. The more adept I am at letting go, the more able I am to live in the moment and appreciate my Soul's immortal perspective.

The bend in the river, the closed door,

they serve your Soul's curriculum.

— *Solano*

There is an old Zen parable about a king who lived in Africa. This king had a good and faithful servant. Together they went off on a hunt and the servant, as always, loaded the firearm that the king was to use. One day the firearm was loaded improperly and it exploded, blowing the thumb off of the king's hand.

The king was in a rage, a fit of fury, due to the incompetence of his servant, and so he had the man thrown into jail. There the man remained for nearly a year. During that time the king's life proceeded with all of the many things that a king will do. Once again he went off on a hunt, during which he and his party were attacked and captured by a cannibalistic tribe from a neighboring region. When they took the king back to their territory and began preparing his body for their meal, they discovered that he was missing a thumb. Superstition overcame them — they believed that anything that was not whole was impure and must not be eaten — so they released the king.

It was then that the king remembered his faithful servant. He went to the jail and released him and begged his forgiveness saying, "It is a horrible thing that I have done. What you did saved my life. It is terrible that I have punished you so."

The servant replied, "No it is not. For had you not thrown me into jail I would have been with you on that hunt and both of us would have been eaten."

When you see with your Soul's eyes you know that
everything that you experience is for your growth.
— *Solano*

THE CAUSE OF STRAIN

You have undoubtedly experienced misfortunes in your life. Reflect on the strain that attends such moments. The antidote to that strain is to realize that there have been blessings birthed within the moments of seeming misfortune. Remember not to look on a circumstance and judge it as being inappropriate to your life, or a mistake, or something that is random.

Coming into this lifetime, your Soul's curriculum has called for you to take the broader view, to come to a greater perspective. This includes considering the possibility that something that has detained you from an appointment actually saved your life, or allowed something greater to come to pass, or put you at the right place in the right time for something that you had called for to happen. Most importantly, your Soul's curriculum was being served.

Certainly you could consider this thought just a rationalization, reaching for optimism that is unfounded. But this is not about optimism. This is an acknowledgement that your Soul is unerring. It is moved through Divine Intelligence into the circumstances that you experience, into the meetings that come to pass, into the rise of fortunes, the fall of fortunes, into health and ill health.

Consider one of the most challenging things that human beings experience — the illusion of birth and then apparent decay into old age and ultimately death. This illusion seems very real, yet it is, in fact, one of those things that the Soul elects purposely for the rehearsal that it provides. Every time you witness an apple shrivel, becoming inedible in the process of going from exquisite ripeness into inevitable decay, your mortality is reflected back to you.

When you meet an old friend that you haven't seen for years, you look at their face and you see that there are now lines where once the skin was smooth. There are shadows under the eyes, there is gray at the temple. In such moments what is reflected to you is the process that your altered ego fears. The altered ego then generates emotions of resistance that equate to the strain that you live with day in and day out.

The strain is what must be eradicated. That strain is nothing more than the altered ego striving to pedal backwards, away from what it fears — its inevitable end — being no more — and the inevitable, exquisite realization that you are immortal.

You are evolving every moment. You are gaining ground.

— *Solano*

The Soul is imbued with Divine wisdom. It is your unerring guidance. It is the source of knowingness and intuition. When you dwell in values of compassion, honesty, forthrightness, courage, unconditional love, and generosity, you are in alignment with the Soul's values.

The altered ego looks at everything as a competition. It is constantly seeking to win. "Oh, you look so young." "You are so thin." "You are so rich." "You are so smart." There are many graces that the altered ego likes to believe that it possesses. Yet the altered ego is a never-ending pit of desire. A compliment on a fleeting grace is not what is sought by the Soul.

The scramble for acknowledgement is repeated over and over again in nearly every conversation, in everything that you see and read and that you repeat to yourself in your mind's dialogue about the nature of life as a human in a body.

Any internal strain that you experience comes from wanting to get it right, even if what you are straining to "get right" is being conscious, being awakened, being identified with your Soul. If you can direct the search for approval and comfort toward integration of the altered ego into the Soul's expansive perspective, then you begin to view mortality as a gift, as an exercise of surrender. You can experience your mortality as the means to let go of specific sources of approval, letting go of the demands that you place on yourself. You can replace the sense of loss with an experience that you are gaining wisdom, freedom, and a more expansive life.

With every act of surrender — every time you accept your life as it is, accept the traffic jam, accept the expense you did not expect, accept the medical report — you gain ground. When you embrace what is and assign to it the value that you are gaining ground in your experience of Oneness, you become more supple. You become more identified with the wisdom that allows you to make a quantum leap from your life as you experience it, marked by strain, to a consciousness in which you become the wise one. You become placid not because of denial, but because you have recognized the source of your life force and what it returns to when the altered ego has rendered itself to the altar of the Soul.

Another Zen parable illustrates the Soul's wisdom. There was a man who lived in China and he awoke one day to discover that his prized stallion had run away. And the neighbors all came to offer their condolences. "It is so sad that your prized stallion has run away." And the man said, "Who knows what is good and what is bad."

A few weeks later the stallion returned, bringing with it three wild mares. And all of the neighbors came to wonder at the beauty of these mares and at the man's good fortune. And they said, "How wonderful it is! Your stallion has returned and your riches have increased with these new mares." And the man said, "Who knows what is good and what is bad."

Then one of the mares, in the process of being broken, attacked the man's only son and broke his leg. Well the neighbors, as you can well imagine, all gathered again to offer their condolences. "It is so very sad that your son, your only son, now is lame." The man again replied, "Who knows what is good and what is bad."

Then shortly thereafter, war broke out and all of the young men in the country were conscripted, but not this man's son, because he was lame. And the neighbors all gathered once again, ecstatic for the man and his good fortune.

And, once again, the man replied, "Who knows what is good and what is bad." But he could not help his smile.

Instead of assigning a value to the event — it is tragic, it is wonderful, it is horrible, it is delightful — say to yourself, "It is what is." You are then adopting an observer position. Simply look at what comes with curiosity and with an eye to understanding the larger picture.

What are you thinking?

— *Solano*

THE DOORWAY TO WISDOM

As you become more Soul-identified, what manifests around you refines. If you simply focus on making a great fortune — the intuition, knowledge, creativity, and innovation necessary to that task present themselves. But for many who have incarnated at this time, their desire and mission is first to awaken, to know God, to be intuitive and compassionate, to be a healer. Such goals create greater accessibility to the thoughts and frequencies and desires of others and, at the same moment, their neuroses and fears.

You are a part of this organism called humanity and you are constantly receiving stimuli. It is no virtue if you become so sensitive that you are overwhelmed by the fears, insecurities, illnesses, and processes of decay that characterize the human tribe. The virtue that is appropriate to your life is to awaken.

Such stimuli often result in the altered ego being activated. When you hear the internal voice of doubt or insecurity about your body, income, country, politics, the environment, your children, your animals, stop and ask yourself, "What am I thinking?" When you observe yourself thinking limited thoughts, judgmental thoughts, fear-based thoughts, mortality-based thoughts, pause, move into an observer position, and thank your altered ego for revealing the area where you have room to grow.

Most everyone has habitual anxiety. Recognizing it as a doorway to wisdom will change its effect in your life. Take a moment to review where your anxiety arises. It may be about body image. It may be about the ability to make a living. It may be about relationships. It may be about sex. Ask yourself, "What challenges come up over and over again in my life?" You will instantly have the answer. You know what it is. That is the doorway. If you courageously face that door and walk through it, you will gain ground.

Fear and strain are always based on thought
that is out of the moment.
— *Solano*

WHAT ARE YOU THINKING?

When you find yourself unable to settle into peace or are agitated, ask yourself, "What am I thinking, what is the strain?" Seek it out — perhaps it is in your linear, left-brain mind engaged in addictive thoughts, or perhaps it is in your gut in the form of an emotion, like fear. Or perhaps you are straining to be loved and appreciated, or worse, straining to control someone. What is causing the strain?

This question is another way in which you can interrupt the altered ego in the act of prompting emotions that prevent you from living in the moment in peace. What is the strain? Just asking yourself gives you a chance to step out of it and identify instead with your immortal Soul. This prompts a balance between the left and right hemispheres of your brain.

Regardless of the many therapies, exercises, disciplines, and religions that offer the tools to overcome addictive anxieties, the only resource needed is within you. It is accessed most easily through your growing identity as a Soul. If your anxiety grows from the fear that there is never enough, your Soul wants you to understand that plenty comes not from the physical realm, not from other human beings, not from selling yourself or renting your time to someone else, but from the Soul itself. It is there that the Fields of Plenty exist.

If your anxiety grows out of longing for acknowledgement, wanting to feel accomplished or intelligent or powerful, that fear stems from the belief that you might be judged unworthy of acceptance and face banishment from communal support. Following that fear and identifying its source — the altered ego — allows you to remember that the future concern is out of the moment. Confronting that fear ultimately leads you to the awareness that you need no one else's acknowledgment. Once you have interrupted the altered ego's habitual treadmill of fear and consequence, you are led back to the Soul and to Oneness.

In this process you gain ground. The anxieties that you experience are addictions. An antidote for these anxieties is to continually ask yourself, "What am I thinking?" Become the observer. Through the observer you reaffirm your identity as an immortal Soul.

When you become Soul-identified, a deep peace
settles into your bones.

— *Solano*

Throughout the history of humanity there have been Soul-identified individuals. Most of them achieved this in the final moments of their life, when all of their belongings, their books, their music, their vitality, their youth, their health, had ebbed. Then, despite the loss, a blazing awareness of foreverness engulfed them.

This is the challenge; this is the call of your Soul. There is no need to wait until your final moments to respond. It is for this that you ponder your life and your experiences. It is for this that you seek to be awake. Become aware of the radiant light that you are in this moment. When you do this, the frequency of your body, the frequency that you are drawn to and the frequency that is magnetized to you, will change.

You will then return to your most authentic, most peaceful self. Reflect for just a moment on any time in your life when you felt radiantly peaceful. Not about the time you had some great physical success, but about the moment in your life when a deep peace settled into your bones, when you knew everything was right, just right. There have been those moments when you felt at one with life, with everything. That is what it feels like to be Soul-identified.

The strain that you experience day to day, the strain of striving to stay fit, of striving to be in rapport with your environment, your identity, your gender, even the strain of longing for community or the strain of the constant desire for more, they are all generated by the altered ego. Yet, all of the ideas that the altered ego adopts to

sustain you are fleeting. Building a kingdom here on
Earth is fleeting, as nothing physical is eternal. Only you.
Your true self. Your Soul.

Integration

Assign power to your altered ego

equivalent to its humility.

— *Solano*

INTERRUPTING THE ALTERED EGO

The altered ego tends to insinuate itself into every aspect of your existence, with the notable exception of the deep sleep that does not have rapid eye movement associated with it. Then you are free from the constraints of the altered ego.

Individuals who are deprived of non-REM sleep very rapidly disintegrate in their mental acuity. Over a period of time this deprivation can trigger a slow descent into madness. This is because if the altered ego alone is allowed to run your life, it will literally drive you crazy. It experiences a perpetual insecurity because it alone cannot understand all procedures, all languages, all protocol. It experiences that insecurity and you embrace it as your own — as being part of who you are. The altered ego learns how to move with relative safety and ease through a social circumstance, or work, or school, so the tendency is to assign it more power than is necessary.

Each and every day the altered ego awakens to a list of have-to's, self-judgments, and a limited perspective of the way life is. You turn on the television. There is news of disaster or crisis and your altered ego goes to work. On the physical level your brain triggers hormones in direct response to the emotions generated by the words spoken by your internal voice — which is, all too often, the voice of the altered ego.

One day you hear that a faraway country is on the brink of bankruptcy that may result in a tide of other countries losing value to their currencies, which may in turn cause your own currency to lose value. You find yourself listening to this news and judging it, thinking, "What about my savings, what about my home, my retirement?" — and suddenly you are breathless and in a panic. The body has secreted hormones from the adrenal glands due to fear and insecurity of the projected future crisis. This happens constantly in the course of a day. The stress experienced in your body, the repetition and the familiarity with that circuitry, is what you recognize as your identity.

Interrupting the process is required to end the illusion. You are trained to believe in your limitations. But this is simply a drama you have chosen because you are learning something about yourself in relationship to the Universe. The more you are willing to push your boundaries, the more you are going to learn about yourself. But the altered ego frequently gets involved in the process and before you can push on a boundary, it sets off an alarm and you recoil and fall into a familiar pattern. In that familiar pattern you will deny yourself the opportunity to challenge the patterns. Humility comes with recognizing the frailty of the altered ego. It is then that you are able to embrace your curriculum, and in so doing, interrupt the altered ego in its habituation to strain. In that moment you begin the process of integration.

Now. This moment. Beingness.
This is all you ever need to explore.
— *Solano*

BEING PRESENT

You don't need to know the future. You don't even need to reflect on your past. Yet most of your moments are spent either in future imaginings or in a past recollection, reflecting on something that someone said or a look that they gave you, or reflecting on some mistake you believe you have made, trying to understand the past and trying to plan for your future. The past and the future are now. This moment is it. This is all.

Bringing yourself to this moment, in every moment, interrupts the altered ego and its inclination to run your life. The altered ego's limited view is what repetitiously makes your body feel a certain way. Being present grants you the ability to decide what you want to experience in the moment, a sense of peace, a sense of ease. A sense of being wholly one with all that is. The only thing standing between you and that experience is your identity with the altered ego, the conditioning that you have embraced. Dropping into that blink of an eye before your body begins to respond to the altered ego with a familiar hormonal pattern, say to yourself, "Now. Here. This moment. Now."

Negative emotion is always the result of the altered ego worrying about the past or future. Not this moment. To have a different experience requires retraining yourself to dwell in the present. Be in this moment, this place, this now. It is the direct antidote to careening off into habitual negative emotions.

A dear friend of many years, a gifted healer and body intuitive, found herself feeling stuck — she expressed dissatisfaction with her limited income and uncertainty about where to live. She wanted more than anything to simply dive into her artistic expression. She was ready to challenge her limitations, but needed some guidance. She asked Solano how to achieve this.

"Beloved Woman, so much of your query is answerable by simply planting your feet and letting the energy gather around. What is most called for is presence. That means, simply be present in your life. In that experience of planting your feet, energy can gather around you in an instant if you are truly and deeply present. When one's habit or pattern is to not be planted — but rather looking at the horizon, scanning for what comes next, or wondering if somewhere else things will be better — that pattern, until broken, will suck up the energy and cut off the deepening roots that have just begun to grow.

Being present allows you to feel, really feel, who you are, in your most native state. It allows you to notice what gifts you have to give, and the gifts that others offer who appear in your life in a moment of need. Half of the battle is simply being present with who you are — in your frequency — and not trying to alter that into a form or format; not trying to force it into a job or career that gives you the imagined comfort of more income, but robs you of true sustenance.

If income was all that mattered, you could attend to that task alone and settle it. If art was all that mattered, you could give yourself to that and live in one basic room with your artist supplies. But you are actually straining for something else. And the strain itself is what prevents it. Completely embrace who you are, what you know or don't know; completely accept your path.

All of your meditations and contemplations and fantasies right now would be well served by seeing, feeling, experiencing deeply the divine law: 'All that comes into manifested reality comes direct from the pure potential and it comes in direct equivalency to your light field.'

In the simplest words, stay where you are and plant your feet. Be present. Embrace what you know about life: love, relationships, the body, the Soul, kindness, compassion, forgiveness, family, courage, inventiveness, aloneness, children, illness, health, the list could go on and on.

Plant your feet. Be present where you are. Your presence will open doors, because of how you will feel about yourself and how that will translate in your body and your light field to the community that surrounds you."

Fully inhabiting the moment grants you the ability to choose which emotions you engage.

— *Solano*

REPETITIVE EMOTION

Consider the issue upon which you repetitively stumble. You choose to feel that repetitive emotion. You continue to work the formula over and over again. What more is there for you to learn about it? You have turned it every way but loose. Turn it loose.

The altered ego continues to work the puzzle, determined that surely if you take that thing, that insecurity, that fear, that anger, that pain, that desire for control, and run the pattern one more time, you will come up with the key to the puzzle, the clue that will free you from it. The altered ego does not have the key. It is a part of your life because it has a task to perform. It is responsible for the many details of communication, human to human. It is through its understanding of convention and protocol that you are recognizable as being part of the human species.

Let the altered ego serve in that capacity. Let it perform the "How do you do" and "Thank you very much" and "No, I'd rather not." The job it does well is negotiating personhood. It knows words. It knows procedure. And it knows through words how to generate often-challenging emotions.

The key to achieving the ability to choose which emotions you engage and which you do not is accomplished
by fully inhabiting the moment. Instead, what usually
happens is that you identify with the altered ego and you
tumble along in your procedural life. You are caught up
in your thoughts. You are caught up in a world that your
altered ego is creating that has nothing to do with what
is. Turn it loose, let go of the attachment to the repetitive
emotions from which you have derived your identity.

Balancing the brain is the key to dwelling
as radiant Soul in mortal form.

— *Solano*

CORPUS CALLOSUM

To further understand the integration of the altered ego with the Soul's grace and wisdom, it is important to understand the function of the corpus callosum, the bridge between the left and the right hemisphere of the human brain.

The two hemispheres of the brain are in charge of different faculties and functions. In an individual whose corpus callosum is well-developed, both hemispheres of the brain are relatively balanced. In such an individual, it is easier to migrate from the left brain where the altered ego's worry, fearfulness, and linear problem-solving takes place — to the right hemisphere, the part of the brain that is more

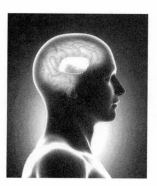

accessible to intuition and the subtler vibratory frequencies. In the right brain, time and space disappear and you have access to knowledge, inspiration, innovation, visions, the wisdom of those who are on the other side, the wisdom of animals, plants, and the Earth itself.

EXERCISE TO ACTIVATE THE CORPUS CALLOSUM

Take a pen in your left hand, even if you are left-handed, and write your name. It is not important to move fast. You do not have to make it beautiful; simply write your name. Now, draw a picture of a dog. It can be a stick figure or more elaborate. If you are having difficulty, simply doodle with your left hand, letting it flow freely, perhaps making circles or erratic movements on the paper.

Now close your eyes and feel your brain. Do not listen to its thoughts, but feel into it. You may feel that there is a pulsing mid-brain. For some the right brain will feel as though it is activated. And it is because you have prompted the corpus callosum to send messages across the mid-line of your brain.

This occurs as well in the yogic breathing practice *nadi shodhana*, which is an alternate nostril breathing practice. Close off the right nostril and breathe in through the left. Close the left and open the right. Breathe out completely and back in through the right, close it off and open the left. Breathe out and back in through the left and continue in that fashion for several rounds. This inspires balance between the hemispheres of the brain as well and it stimulates the activity in the corpus callosum.

Any time you find yourself too much in the dialogue with the linear brain, the altered ego mind, stop. Actually say to that part of your being, "Stop. Stop talking. Stop worrying. Stop." If you have access to paper and pen, pick up the pen in your left hand and simply begin to write or doodle or draw because it will begin to energize the corpus callosum and the right brain. If you can close your eyes and engage *nadi shodhana*, do. If you can accomplish none of these things, then simply ask yourself the question, "What am I thinking?" Then pause and listen and feel the answer. This will provide you the ability to step back from the thoughts.

Stepping back from your thoughts, direct yourself to move across the bridge from left brain to right brain. Be literal in directing your body, and center your thoughts in the right hemisphere. Over 98% of all human bodies are oriented with the right hemisphere of the brain being responsible for the following functions:

• feeling

• imagination

• symbols and images

• present and future

• philosophy and religion

• "getting it" (understanding deeper meaning)

• appreciation

• spatial perception

To further access your association to the functions of the right brain, imagine a radiant light in the center of your chest, and imagine that that radiant light is your immortal self, the divine wisdom that dwells within you. That imagining takes place in the right brain, the creative brain, the brain that can provide access to everything in the Universe because time and space are illusions.

Non-linear mind is responsible for every leap of
consciousness that has taken place.
— *Solano*

The altered ego will have the incentive to integrate with your Soul when your life begins to become more graceful and it begins to identify with a more expansive state of consciousness. This occurs when you continually bring yourself back to the present moment.

Recognize that the genesis of every emotion and every structure that is built between you and another person or other people, is right within you. By observing the altered ego's conditioning, and informing the altered ego that that conditioning is not who you are, you begin the process of integrating the altered ego and your Soul. You are immortal, Infinite Intelligence. Fear, insecurity, doubt, worry, anger — all these are products of your thoughts.

You feel these limited emotions because the altered ego has conditioned you to believe that your life as you experience it through your emotions is who you are. The consequence of living at the effect of your emotions is evident in negative experiences and setbacks. By the time you get to that point in your life, the altered ego is so confused that sustaining a simple thought of abundance or unconditional love, a simple thought of joy or forever-ness, is difficult at best. But you, identified with your Soul, can make this your state of consciousness.

Place your Soul in the greatest position of empowerment.

— *Solano*

CHAIN OF COMMAND

It comes down to assigning a chain of command. Reflect
again on the relationship that you identified between you
and another individual in which there is not a free flow of
unconditional love. How different would it be for you if you
actually changed your chain of command so that your Soul
was in command of your point of view, your heart, your
expression, your throat, in command of all of the hormones
of your body, and then engage that relationship? The first
thing that would change is that your heart wouldn't close.
The structures that are built between you and others that
inhibit the free flow of energy are created because the heart
closes.

The linear mind must be informed by the Soul's greater
wisdom. That requires your patience, your willfulness to
actually be in the moment, to notice the structures that are
built between you and another person and to acknowledge
that they are not built by the Soul, but rather by the altered
ego.

EXERCISE TO ESTABLISH CHAIN OF COMMAND

Take a deep breath. Close your eyes. Stimulate the right hemisphere of your brain by rubbing the index finger and thumb of your left hand together. Imagine yourself far above the planet. At this distance, you gain a perspective free from the many details of earthly existence. That is the Soul's viewpoint. And now look from that perspective at your life. Look particularly at that emotion, that stumbling block that you come up against again and again. Does it not simply dissolve, seated in that beingness? Breathe deeply into your body and give thanks to your altered ego for its service, and affirm your chain of command with the Soul in the position of primacy this moment.

THE RIGHT BRAIN

The more that you can dwell in your right brain, identified with your Soul, the more you challenge the altered ego's experience of singularity and the strain that accompanies singularity. Then, gaining ground is not just a moment in which you happily discover that you are becoming more adept as a master of manifestation. Rather, you begin to dwell consistently in the Fields of Plenty by coming to your simple, pure identity as an immortal — the identity of yourself as forever and always one with God the Source.

When you find yourself caught in a limited vision of your life — the key is to be able to migrate to an identity where you recognize that the body is but clothing that you will eventually shed. *You* go on, forever gathering wisdom through experience.

You are, in fact, all that is. There is no distinction between you and the furthest reaches of the universe. You *are* the universe.

Fields of Plenty

Everything is pure potential.
You, as a Soul, dwell in Fields of Plenty.
— *Solano*

What appears to be solid is energy. It is potential. There is potential all around you. The three dimensional world appears to be solid and real, yet it is simply waves of energy that have assembled around you in agreement with your consciousness so that you might inhabit this dreamscape. As you begin to understand the illusion of solidity and come to know it as energy with pure potential, you begin to move into the knowledge that you dwell every moment in Fields of Plenty.

Here, in this collective consciousness — this set of agreements that define time and space — new coastlines and new mountains are built bit by bit — one grain of sand at a time. You dwell not simply in the present as radiant immortal Soul, you dwell as a Soul *and* as a projected self — an altered ego. It is because of that blended consciousness that you experience change as incremental rather than instantaneous.

Sometimes your altered ego is in charge and sometimes you bring yourself back to the consciousness that understands that you contain everything within you, the potential for any manifestation.

The Soul understands that if you utter a command, knowing that you are pure potential and all that surrounds you *is* you, then the medium that you dwell in organizes itself around that consciousness and what you have commanded comes to be.

The idea of "command" conjures up images of an obedient dog and his master or a general and his troops. Taking command can be an uncomfortable concept. In one of Solano's earlier teachings he asked, "If you suddenly understood that you are God and could destroy worlds and create entirely new ones with a simple thought, would you be responsible enough not to succumb to the temptations inherent in such power?" *There have been times when I exercised command and proclaimed this or that thing to be "mine, NOW" only to have nothing apparent happen. What if my commands were in direct opposition to another Soul's command? We are both Divine Intelligence — who wins?*

So I asked for clarification on this particular concept. Solano replied: "The key is to know that you are pure potential. Do you know this in every moment? Do you know that all that surrounds you, which includes other sentient beings, is you? If everything around you IS you, how does that inform what you ask for, and how you behave? Quite literally you must first know that when you make a command it must be spoken in such impeccable harmony and compassion for all that there is no resistance; rather, the pure potential is already aware of the requirement and, as such, is primed to provide it. It is YOU, then, anticipating your own need that provides that which you command."

This explanation took it out of the realm of individual wants or needs. Thinking of "command" as coming from an integrated place where the command is correct for the whole of creation is something that begins to be more understandable.

The Infinite Potential, in which you dwell,

provides all that you require.

— *Solano*

There was once a kindly old man who dwelled in a forest. He lived simply in a cottage in harmony with the land. If he took the life of a creature for his food, he asked permission to do so, knowing fully that the Creator God had created all that was, in order to provide for all that is. If he had to take a tree for fire, likewise he would ask permission of the tree and of the forest and of the consciousness there, that he could take that tree to keep himself warm in his little cottage.

The Earth Spirits, the intelligent consciousness of the forest, were grateful for this Soul who dwelled among them, who honored them and loved them, living harmoniously with them. And so they blessed his little cottage, and particularly they blessed the barrel in which he kept ale so that it became an unending supply. There was always ale whenever he opened the spigot. It was a bounty he never questioned. It simply was. And so it went for years, until one day the old woman who came to tend his cottage from time to time became curious about this. She asked the man how it was that he never went to buy ale, yet there was always ale in his barrel. The old man only shrugged and walked away. And so she went to the barrel and opened it to look inside. What she found was nothing but cobwebs and spiders. And she cried out to the old man, "There is nothing there! The barrel is empty. What will you do now?"

A look of panic crept over his face as he peered into the empty cask. From then on whenever the spigot was opened, nothing came from the barrel.

When the altered ego proclaims that there is lack, it has an impact on the individual's experience of the flow of abundance that comes from the Soul's understanding that pure potential surrounds you at all times.

There is no secret to achieving abundance.

— *Solano*

Plenty is your birthright and you manifest your plenty in every moment. What we have examined here is the gap between your radiant immortal self and the altered ego that frequently operates your body. That self, the altered ego, judges, and believes its own story. It believes that if you think hard enough and if you are clever enough and if you turn your intellect to problem solving long enough, you will be able to crack the nut and find happiness and success.

But when the altered ego that is indoctrinated to this realm of time and space is doing the thinking and trying to solve the problems, you are going to wind up with a barrel full of cobwebs and spiders. Because that limited self looks to your pocketbook and sees it empty, or looks in your bed and sees no lover there, or looks at your body and sees advancing age or ill health. It is that consciousness that believes these experiences are reality, adding another grain of sand to the mountain of belief in lack and singularity.

All the while, the radiant immortal consciousness that you are gazes out on the Fields of Plenty and sees and knows that you are given all that you require. In fullness. Every moment.

The Fields of Plenty are within, in equal measure for all. They are provided equally for a beggar on the streets of Delhi as they are for someone living in South Hampton, because it is not about a bank account, a car, or a new television. It is not about getting stronger, more svelte, and healthier. It is about you understanding that you dwell every moment as an immortal Soul. That is who you are, not separate from all that is.

If an individual comes into a lifetime as a captain of industry, and another individual comes in as a beggar, one is not more advanced than the other. They simply have come into different aspects of their Soul's desire for wisdom to be satisfied by that particular experience. The Soul does not judge a lifetime in which the altered ego experiences profound lack and hunger, or violence, or the pain of being objectified. In such a lifetime, even if the individual does not remember that they are immortal, all that the Soul knows is unending supply and immortality.

The Soul only knows what you have come here to gain — wisdom and understanding as a unique Soul growing into the greater consciousness of the One. Your Soul is always and ever aware that there is no lack — only plenty.

Turn your eyes once again to the great ocean
of intelligence and merge with it.

— *Solano*

You have been granted, like a droplet of water, the ability to perceive yourself as singular. Nevertheless, you are One with the great ocean of pure potential, Divine Intelligence. You are simple Is-ness. You are following your Soul's mandate for growth, and that growth ultimately brings you back to where, as that single droplet, you once again return to the great ocean and merge with it, full of your awareness of singularity and fuller still of your awareness of Oneness.

When you are still and you find yourself basking in your essential radiance, identification with your body falls away and your altered ego quiets. In that moment there is only One. In that moment you merge with countless others who have experienced singularity, but inhabit Oneness.

The moment has come when the altered ego can no longer have its way in your life, because you are diligently seeking to live your Soul's values. Now the scales are tipping. You are beginning to recognize the difference between the altered ego operating your body and the experience of dwelling in the radiance.

When you dwell identified with the Soul, you understand that this moment, whatever your life is, is abundance — is "plenty." This moment, what is, is fullness. This moment, what is, allows you through your identification with that radiance, to understand the pliability of all that surrounds you. It is that knowledge and the diligence of witnessing and observing that allows you then to fully identify with that which witnesses — your radiant, immortal Soul.

ABOUT THE AUTHOR

LD Thompson was born in Indiana and educated at
Alaska Pacific University and Indiana University.

In his twenties, a profound mystical
experience signaled the beginning
of his spiritual journey. As a result
of that experience, he dedicated his
life to integrating the wisdom he
received and sharing it with others.

LD is an inspirational speaker,
filmmaker, and professor of film and video production
at College of the Desert. His first book, *The Message: A
Guide to Being Human*, has been translated into German.
His writing also appears in the anthology *A Fuller View:
Buckminster Fuller's Vision of Hope and Abundance for
All*. As well, LD is a contributor to *The Huffington Post*,
and various print and online magazines.

LD travels the world speaking and presenting workshops
and seminars. He balances his time between the Sonoran
Desert in California and Europe.

For more information, please visit:
www.ldthompson.com

DIVINE
ARTS

HERE ARE OTHER **DIVINE ARTS** BOOKS YOU MAY ENJOY

THE SACRED SITES OF THE DALAI LAMAS
Glenn H. Mullin   2013 Nautilus Silver Medalist

"As this most beautiful book reveals, the Dalai Lamas continue to teach us that there are, indeed, other ways of thinking, other ways of being, other ways of orienting ourselves in social, spiritual, and ecological space."
— **Wade Davis, Explorer-in-Residence, National Geographic Society**

THE SHAMAN & AYAHUASCA: *Journeys to Sacred Realms*
Don José Campos   2013 Nautilus Silver Medalist

"This remarkable and beautiful book suggests a path back to understanding the profound healing and spiritual powers that are here for us in the plant world. This extraordinary book shows a way toward reawakening our respect for the natural world, and thus for ourselves."
— **John Robbins, author, *The Food Revolution* and *Diet for a New America***

A HEART BLOWN OPEN: *The Life & Practice of Zen Master Jun Po Denis Kelly Roshi*
Keith Martin-Smith   2013 Nautilus Silver Medalist

"This is the story of our time... an absolute must-read for anyone with even a passing interest in human evolution..."
— **Ken Wilber, author, *Integral Spirituality***

"This is the legendary story of an inspiring teacher that mirrors the journey of many contemporary Western seekers."
— **Alex Grey, artist and author of *Transfigurations***

SOPHIA—THE FEMININE FACE OF GOD: *Nine Heart Paths to Healing and Abundance*
Karen Speerstra   2013 Nautilus Gold Medalist

"Karen Speerstra shows us most compellingly that when we open our hearts, we discover the wisdom of the Feminine all around us. A totally refreshing exploration, and beautifully researched read."
— **Michael Cecil, author, *Living at the Heart of Creation***

NEW BELIEFS NEW BRAIN: *Free Yourself from Stress and Fear*
Lisa Wimberger

"Lisa Wimberger has earned the right, through trial by fire, to be regarded as a rising star among meditation teachers. No matter where you are in your journey, New Beliefs, New Brain will shine a light on your path."
— **Marianne Williamson, author, *A Return to Love* and *Everyday Grace***

THE MESSAGE: *A Guide to Being Human*
LD Thompson

"Simple, profound, and moving! The author has been given a gift... a beautiful way to distill the essence of life into an easy-to-read set of truths, with wonderful examples along the way. Listen... for that is how it starts."
— Lee Carroll, author, the *Kryon* series; co-author, *The Indigo Children*

A FULLER VIEW: *Buckminster Fuller's Vision of Hope and Abundance for All*
L. Steven Sieden

"This book elucidates Buckminster Fuller's thinking, honors his spirit, and creates an enthusiasm for continuing his work."
— Marianne Williamson, author, *Return To Love* and *Healing the Soul of America*

2500 YEARS OF WISDOM: *Sayings of the Great Masters*
D.W. Brown

The wisdom of the greatest minds on earth. All in one place.
This book of carefully selected and arranged quotations represents the greatest philosophical thoughts mankind has produced in its attempt to come to a deeper understanding of the human condition.

WRITING FROM THE INSIDE OUT: *The Practice of Freeform Writing*
Stephen Lloyd Webber

"I urge others to write from the heart to find their true artistic voice. Here is a book that profoundly helps one explore that mysterious personal journey. A navigation guide to our inner creative magic."
— Pen Densham, screenwriter, *Robin Hood: Prince of Thieves* and *Moll Flanders*

CHANGE YOUR STORY, CHANGE YOUR LIFE: *A Path to Success*
Jen Grisanti

"It turns out you can actually get a handle on your life problems by approaching them as an ongoing story that you can rewrite and direct for a better effect."
— Christopher Vogler, author, *The Writer's Journey*

HEAL YOUR SELF WITH WRITING
Catherine Ann Jones

"An elixir for the soul"
— *Psychology Today*

"This is so much more than a book on writing. It is a guide to the soul's journey, with Catherine Ann Jones as a compassionate teacher and wise companion along the way."
— Dr. Betty Sue Flowers, Series Consultant/Editor, *Joseph Campbell and the Power of Myth*

Divine Arts sprang to life fully formed as an intention to bring spiritual practice into daily life.

Human beings are far more than the one-dimensional creatures perceived by most of humanity and held static in consensus reality. There is a deep and vast body of knowledge — both ancient and emerging — that informs and gives us the understanding, through direct experience, that we are magnificent creatures occupying many dimensions with untold powers and connectedness to all that is.

Divine Arts books and films explore these realms, powers, and teachings through inspiring, informative, and empowering works by pioneers, artists, and great teachers from all the wisdom traditions. We invite your participation and look forward to learning how we may serve you.

Onward and upward,
Michael Wiese, Publisher